"You are the light at the end of the tunnel. I ask that you collectively come together in the higher Ascension agreement and download the frequency of Love, Light, peace, harmony and equality for all people"

~ Message from Archangel Michael ~

The Creator Archangels & Masters Speak on the Cosmic Ascension

& the Light at the End of the Tunnel

Michelle Phillips

Creator material channeled by Michelle Phillips
Copyright © 2011, 2012, 2016 by Michelle Phillips

All rights reserved. No part of this book may be reproduced or copied by any mechanical, photographic, or electronic process, or in the form of an audio recording, or otherwise be copied for public or private use without the written permission from the author.

Michelle Phillips
Sedona, AZ
(928) 821-2038
www.soulsawakening.com

ISBN 978-1541379763

Printed in the United States of America

Cover art and book design by Mark Gelotte.
www.markgelotte.com

DEDICATION

I dedicate this book to my mother, Norma Vivian Macnab. This year I had the privilege and honor of assisting her home into Spirit.

Because of my spirituality and spiritual work, accessing the spirit world is very easy for me.

I knew my mother had a fear of death, of the unknown, and I wanted to be with her so she would feel safe as she left this world through the birth canal home into Spirit.

My mother and I had a very karmic relationship. Our journey together here on Earth was not easy.

Now, as I reflect on our life together, I can see the humor in our Soul's agreement. She was actually one of my greatest teachers. Thank you, mom.

My mother was a very strong woman, a survivor. She basically raised five children by herself. Our father was a World War II veteran and had PTSD. He was a big man and because of his size carried a gun in the front lines of the war.

Back then, not much was known about PTSD. Because of his condition, our life was an emotional roller coaster ride. We moved every year, often twice a year. I went to a different school every year, sometimes two schools in a year.

My Mother always kept it together for us; many times she worked two jobs to support us. She was definitely the matriarch of our family. She left this world at the age of 92 surrounded in love with my sister, Melody, myself and her husband, John, who was 27 years her junior.

My mother definitely did things her way. She and John had a

beautiful love story. They were married for 27 years and together for 30. They showed us that love is the only truth. Age made no difference in their journey together.

On her birthday, October 28th, all five of us (kids) would come together to celebrate her. This began on her 70th birthday until her passing at the age of 92.

My mother was a stunningly beautiful, elegant woman. She had a great sense of humor and could tell a joke that would stop you in your tracks.

I got my strength and survival instincts from my mother. She never gave up; she just kept pushing through life.

When I was younger, I could not see our difficult relationship as a gift.

It was when I started my own healing journey that I could really experience my cup full instead of empty. My mother was the greatest catalyst in my life for change. At that time in my life, I could not imagine coming back to the Earth again with her in such difficult roles.

Because of my childhood hurt from our relationship, I started looking for ways to heal, and through healing my own inner child I received the gift of how to assist others to heal their inner children.

I can honestly say that of the many gifts I have received from my mother, the gift of assisting her home was the greatest heart opening love experience in my life. We had about a week together in total love.

Our karmic journey had come to an end; we had come full circle. We were complete. Our hearts opened and became one heart.

A couple of days before she left, I asked her if she needed anything, and she looked into my eyes and into my soul and said, "Just you, sweetheart, and I really mean it." Those were the words I had been waiting to hear and feel my whole life. We were complete. We had come home together in love.

When I think of her, which is often, all I can feel is our love in the last few days of her life.

As she left this world, she gave me a gift of a re-birth. We were birthed together beyond our earthly journey and into our One heart of eternal love.

Thank you my beautiful Mother for giving birth to me and for re-birthing me again into love and for allowing me to be a midwife to birth you out of this world and home into Spirit, into the One heart of love.

All we need is love, and our whole journey in this lifetime is to love ourselves enough to return home into the One heart of love.

We individually and collectively are going through a death of karma. We are shifting through many Ascension portals and into a magnificent re-birth of ourselves to awaken and Co-Create Heaven on Earth.

And I say to all of you, my Soul brothers and sisters, from my heart and Soul to yours: "All I need is you, sweetheart, and I really mean it."

We are truly a gift to one another. The time to share our love, honor and gratitude of each other is now.

Thank you, mom, and all of you.

I love you and I honor you for your agreement to come to the Earth at this incredible time of our collective Souls Awakening. I am very grateful that our paths have crossed in this lifetime.

    Thank You. Namaste, Michelle

Acknowledgements

I want to acknowledge Julie Carey who has typed and edited all four of my books. I write my books long hand and Julie then types and edits my transcripts. She can read my handwriting better than I can. She is very flexible, quick and joyful to work with.

I am also very grateful for Mark Gelotte, my graphic artist. He has co-created the artwork for each of my books and finalizes the print copy. The Creator and my spiritual team show me the vision of the covers and illustrations for the books, and Mark using his intuition, brings the pictures to life. He is very humble, creative and tuned in to Spirit and the energies of the messages, downloads and illustrations brought through me.

I want to thank my good friend and confidant of almost 30 years, Diana Urbas. I would call Diana every morning after the spiritual transmissions were downloaded through me. Together we would feel and experience the DNA activations and energies of the downloads. Diana, a former English teacher, has edited and assisted others with their books and willingly offered me her expertise.

I honor my spiritual team for downloading this book through me so quickly. Spirit's intention for these DNA activated messages is to assist the masses to move from fear into the higher purpose of this incredible collective Souls Awakening and into the Oneness of Love: "The Light at the end of the Tunnel."

Michelle's Introduction

This book is a total surprise to me. I had made up my mind not to do another book because of how much time, energy and expense it takes to put a book out into the world.

One morning while standing in my kitchen, Archangel Michael came up behind me and asked if I would channel a transmission that he wanted to share with the world.

Of course, I lovingly agreed. Archangel Michael is a big part of my spiritual team. To feel, see and hear Michael around me is very common.

His transmission gave me a great sense of peace and harmony. My heart opened and became One with his. My whole body filled with so much love, and I felt a sense of safety for myself and our world. I was immediately vibrating in the higher picture of our world with Michael and the other Archangels and Masters. We were looking down at our world, and I experienced the collective agreement that we are all going through.

I could see and feel many beautiful colors in and around our world. I was shown many Ascension codings, patterns and portals that we are collectively birthing ourselves through. I was also being shown that we are exactly where we have collectively agreed to be, to assist us and our world beyond duality and into the One heart and One love in which we were first created.

We are coming home together, and all of the chaos in world is the collective shadow awakening and being exposed so that it can play itself out.

Our agreement as the light carriers is to align our thoughts, emotions, feelings and inner light with the Masters, Archangels and The Creator.

As we are ascending, our collective light has activated all of our own karmic emotions as well as the collective, karmic emotions of our world and all worlds.

As I was being shown this, I could see and feel that we are right on target with our world's Ascension. We have so many light Beings from all dimensions and Creations that are assisting us on our journey through the Ascension portals into Enlightenment and into the One Cell or Soul of Creation in which we were first created.

I was also shown our world's future, our New Earth where we are living in peace, harmony, love and equality for all.

I witnessed that many of the amazing children coming to our planet now are Masters and Angels being born fully conscious. They are the hope and future of our world. Their agreement is to open portals of light into higher dimensions by being the heart and wings of love from the higher consciousness.

I could see thousands and thousands of Beings with beautiful, colorful wings flowing around our world as they were waiting for the exact moment to incarnate into our world.

As they were flowing together around our world, they were building a field, or safety net, around our planet.

I could see that the light of their Being was opening portals of beautiful music and sound that was harmonizing with the colors, songs and sounds of us who already inhabit the Earth.

As they incarnate through their mothers, they are bringing the fully conscious energy and frequencies of light with them. They become the portals of light and higher consciousness that are the future of our world.

As we are ascending through time, we are awakening through ourselves multi-dimensionally.

Our own light is activating and clearing old energy and

patterns that no longer serve us in the highest. The same is true for our collective Souls Awakening.

After Archangel Michael's transmission, I sat in silence and in awe of the magnitude of what we have collectively agreed to go through. Because I was vibrating with Spirit in such high frequencies, I could not feel my physical body. I had merged with my light body.

The next morning while standing in the kitchen, Archangel Michael once again appeared and asked me to download another transmission.

As I started channeling the transmission, I realized it was not from Michael; it was from Archangel Gabriel. When I was finished with the transmission, I started writing down names of Masters and Archangels and even a title. When I finished and looked at what I had written, I laughed to myself. "Oh my God, this is a book!"

After the initial shock, I sat down every morning and brought messages through from different Archangels, Masters and The Creator.

All of their messages bring the energies and DNA activations of the higher picture of what is being played out on our planet now. The downloads activate our DNA systems into our higher selves, into the higher self of Gaia, our beautiful Mother Earth and into the higher self of God, of Creation.

Their messages give us hope for our future and the future of our World and planet. The higher frequencies of their messages activate our DNA systems into the frequencies of the higher master plan of our collective Souls Awakening and Ascension.

Some of the messages brought to you in the book speak of experiences of Creation that you might not quite understand.

In the first book I channeled from The Creator, these

experiences were explained in depth. For that reason I have inserted three chapters from "The Creator Speaks" in the back of this book. You can refer to these chapters to have a greater understanding of what the Masters and Archangels are sharing with you

I am honored to bring to you the messages and energies that the Archangels, Masters and The Creator have brought through. Their intention is to shift you from fear and into the greater awakening and understanding of the greatest roles that have ever been played out on the beautiful planet Earth.

This great, spiritual team wanted their DNA activated messages to reach you and our world very quickly, to move you into peace, harmony, love, grace and Oneness.

For that reason this manuscript and book came through me and was finished in about six weeks.

Relax and enjoy the beautiful messages and downloads being given to you from Spirit.

I thank you. I love you and honor you for your willingness to incarnate onto this beautiful planet in our great, collective Souls Awakening.

In love, light, gratitude and grace,

Michelle Phillips

Contents

Dedication v

Acknowledgements ix

Michelle's Introduction xi

CHAPTER ONE
Mother/Father Creator 1

CHAPTER 2
Ashtar of the Galactic Command 6

CHAPTER 3
Archangel Michael's Transmission #1 15

CHAPTER 4
Archangel Michael's Transmission #2 18

CHAPTER 5
Archangel Michael's Transmission #3 23

CHAPTER 6
Light Walkers Among Us 27

CHAPTER 7
Lemurians Speaking – Love's Awakening 30

CHAPTER 8
Jeshua 34

CHAPTER 9
Magdalene Speaks 42

CHAPTER 10
Archangel Uriel Speaks 49

CHAPTER 11
The Creator Speaks: Our Collective Souls Awakening 57

CHAPTER 12
Archangel Raphael Speaks 63

CHAPTER 13
The Creator Speaks: The Light at the End of the Tunnel 69

CHAPTER 14
Quan Yin 77

CHAPTER 15
Gaia 85

CHAPTER 16
Mother Earth 89

CHAPTER 17
Archangel Gabriel Speaks 95

CHAPTER 18
St. Germain / I AM-Violet Flame 98

CHAPTER 19
The Creator Speaks: Re-building a New World – Riding the Waves of Freedom 104

CHAPTER 20
The Creator Speaks: Co-Creating Heaven on Earth 109

CHAPTER 21
Coming Home – Through Intention 114

CHAPTER 22
The Creator Speaks: Mirroring Your Self-Love to Freedom 118

CHAPTER 23
The Creator Speaks: Seasons of Your Inner Awakenings 122

CHAPTER 24
I AM 128

APPENDIX I
Jeshua and Magdalene's Love Story 132

APPENDIX 2
The Planet Maldek and the Soul of Mother Earth 149

The Creator's Story of Maldek 158

APPENDIX 3
Mother & Father Earth's 2012 Reunion 167

About the Author 179

CHAPTER ONE

Mother/Father Creator

I am the light of your Being. We glow together in the center of all consciousness. We have always been. You have never been separate from Me because you are Me.

You began with Me and will return to Me.

I know this lifetime that you have chosen to inhabit now seems a bit challenging. It is challenging because you have stretched your Soul's consciousness to the beginning of your existence as well as the end of your existence coming back home into the One heart of love, of our One Creation.

You have come full circle. Not just one circle but many circles of completion. As I exist through all consciousness, so do you because you are Me – We are One consciousness that blends through all Creation.

You have seen the world through the eyes of your karmic lessons, and now you are experiencing your world and beyond through your spiritual eye; your third eye. All of your eyes are blending together and shifting you into My eyes and heart and into the larger picture of Our One Creation.

You are now experiencing Me through Our One heart. This is somewhat challenging because Our One heart is constant ebb and flow. In Our heart's eye, there is nothing to hang onto. There is constant shifting; shifting of your belief systems, of patterns, and of your old, karmic foundations.

As you look at the cycles of your world, there is not one sunset or sunrise that is the same. The seasons of your world are constantly shifting. Have you ever seen one summer, winter, spring, or autumn that is the exact duplicate of its last season? It does not exist. Every season is constantly dying and re-birthing itself. Summer, winter, spring and fall do not stop to think about what they are going to do when its season comes around again.

They go with the flow of life: Death – Re-birth. A season does not feel bad, rejected, hurt, abandoned or pass blame that another season is more beautiful or has more time or that people like it best. It is the season of Creation, just as your Soul has the seasons of Creation within you.

Life cycles will always take you through death and rebirth. Your Soul's re-birth now is the birth of your re-incarnation into this lifetime. Through your lifetimes, you will experience many of your own cycles of death and re-birth. Death of belief systems, death of relationships, death of children, death of the way things were or the way you want them to be. Death of your hopes and dreams, death of your ideals, death of beliefs of religions, and always, always, always there is a re-birth. When one cycle ends, there is always a re-birth of your Soul's next learning experience.

Your children, loved ones, and relationships that may have left you went into a re-birth of their Soul's next lessons, which catapulted you into the birth of your next lesson.

Your children and loved ones came home to be back into the heart of love.

They did not leave you. They will always be a part of your heart. Their departure opened a portal of light (It may not seem like light at the time.) for the next step of your Soul's journey. The next step may be to experience grief and loss that you could not imagine to be possible. As you move through the grief, many times you feel anger and injustice, and from this start looking for answers and ways to heal beyond your old belief systems, patterns, or religions.

Many times you took life for granted, and from this unimaginable loss, or grief, you started choosing to live your life - to feel your life - and from this desire, you chose to assist others who have gone through similar situations. Your re-birth led you into your Soul's higher purpose and into the gift of leading many into the light of their Being.

There is no death, just a constant ebb and flow and a re-birth of the next cycle of your Soul's journey.

The same experience of death and re-birth happens when you or someone you love becomes sick or ill.

You lose your foundation, what you thought was real - another death and re-birth of your belief systems, illusions and emotions.

The last death on the Earth is when you physically leave your earthly body and return home to Me. Your re-birth will be glorious as the Angels blow their trumpets and assist you home through a doorway of light, of total love, forgiveness, gratitude, compassion and Oneness.

All of your illusional stories dissolve into love. You will experience the joy and happiness of all of your loved ones that have come home into love before you.

You will move into the larger picture of your Soul's earthly journey and in one instance experience all that you have gone through in its divinity, perfection and love!

The gift of this earthly lifetime is you don't have to wait until you physically die; you can experience the glorious re-birth of infinite love within yourself now.

The veils of illusion are dissolving, and many of you are

actually having what you call near death experiences. You are temporarily leaving, and expanding your mental, emotional, cellular and physical body's consciousness into higher dimensions of love. Through this re-birth you understand that love heals all, and when you move back into Earth's dimensional realities, you are still very open to the miracles of healing - mentally, emotionally and physically – the healing that love expands you into.

Because you are the Cells of each other, you actually open portals of light, of love, for others to expand and awaken into. From this place a re-birth of your dreams and goals shift you into a higher lens of perception and into wanting for your world what you want for yourself. You truly start experiencing yourself as One Cell/Soul of Creation.

Your heart and mind blend into My heart and mind, and together We unfold the collective into higher dimensions of love for all. This love starts shifting your world through the Ascension portals and gives all the opportunity to awaken into love, hope, forgiveness, gratitude and Oneness. Many of you are having spontaneous awakenings and rememberings of who you are multi-dimensionally. Every moment your world's collective DNA systems are breaking down old control systems of greed, fear, and hopelessness.

This is a death and re-birth cycle of control. This is creating uncertainty and imbalance. There has always been an imbalance; the veils are just now being lifted. Through intention, as a collective consciousness, you can shift your world into balance.

How do you do this? By staying connected to Sophia, My heart, and Me, the Creator. We do not fear; remember, in higher dimensions there is only love. As you and I become one love beyond time, I will guide you back into Heaven on Earth.*

All that you see and experience are old, karmic systems breaking down so that as one consciousness We can and will re-birth your world through the karmic death portal and into a balanced world where the male and female dance together in respect and harmony; where the heart and ego become allies; where love is your foundation and flow; where you allow your and My higher purpose to glide all through the seasons of life's existence and back into harmony and grace; where We sing Mother Earth's song of beauty and resonate with the symphony of colors, sound, and music that Mother Earth so willingly and lovingly shares with us; where We move through all time frequencies and back into the harmony and ebb and flow of death and rebirth; where We come home together truly as One Soul of love.

You are never, ever alone. Call on Me, and you will feel a memory of Our love awaken within you. You have many Masters, Angels, Elders, Wayshowers and Animals that are constantly surrounding you and your world as We are gliding you and Mother Earth through the Ascension portal back home into love's Creation.

I love you. I AM you.

Mother/Father Creation

---

*In my first book "The Creator Speaks," The Creator explains how his feminine heart opened: "I had discovered My own self-love from the core of My Being. As I continued to surrender into My core, I knew that My heart awakening was My own feminine, My own beloved, and I called her Sophia. Sophia means My Beloved. The love of my light." (For more information on the Creator's journey of coming into balance with his male and female and all of Creation, refer to "The Creator Speaks" book.)

CHAPTER 2

ASHTAR OF THE GALACTIC COMMAND

This is Ashtar. I and my Galactic Command come to you now as your brothers. We are all on the same team: the team that is assisting the Ascension of the Earth and all inhabitants into the safety of Creation.

We, with my brothers and sisters of light, constantly monitor your world. We are always with you protecting you and your Earth through the Ascension portal into one consciousness of Creation.

Just as you individually are ascending, so is your great Mother Earth. She signed up to be the vehicle to hold all of your Souls while you move though the greatest journey your Soul has ever agreed to go through. This is the lifetime that you individually and collectively have agreed to clear out karmically and clear karmic contracts of fear and separation for the collective.

We are many, from different star systems and even universes that are protecting you and the Earth through this amazing journey of freedom.

We have come together as ONE just as you are coming together as one blended race of many beautiful colors, languages and sounds. This is our agreement as well as yours.

There is nothing to fear of losing your planet. That will not happen.

As I said, our team is constantly monitoring and protecting you from energies that do not have the best interest of your planet.

Your planet is seeded with star Beings from all of Creation, meaning many different dimensional Beings are on your planet assisting to bring it home safely.

Imagine your planet as a live spaceship. We are assisting the ship to glide through all dimensions, all star systems, and home into One Soul. The One Soul is the heart of all other planets that have already ascended.

In your day to day life, imagine the thrill of being on a live spaceship that is gliding through all dimensional time frequencies and that you collectively are the great commanders of this amazing ship.

What glides your ship home is your frequencies, your energies. Your thoughts and actions propel this ship through time portals of all Creation.

Thoughts are energy, and energy is what moves, shifts, and creates your world's collective consciousness. Your collective thoughts and intentions are opening and healing your heart. Your heart's awakening and remembering of love is influencing and changing your thoughts into the higher road - the higher chakra system – of Co-Creation instead of the lower chakras of survival.

As I said, you are not alone and have assistance from many different planetary systems that are holding the light energy for you to merge into your higher remembering.

As you continue to merge into higher frequencies, your subconscious and unconscious minds are clearing, opening, awakening, and aligning into the memories of who you really are, which is a magnificent multi-dimensional Being of light, of Creation.

Many of you are awakening and remembering that you are Masters and Angels that have agreed to lower your frequencies, come down to the Earth and match and merge with many karmic energies and the pain body's influences. As you unravel from the stories of your past experiences from the beginning of your Soul's journey, you unravel the stories for all because you are all.

You were vibrating in a sea of frozen emotions, and through your desires and intentions of love and freedom, you shifted into the breath of life, of love, of the ebb and flow of Creation.

It was through this shift that you merged with your higher self and higher aspects of your Master selves throughout all of Creation.

Through this merge you assisted many to unravel from their stories and into their own breath of multi-dimensionality.

Many of you are aspects of my team, the Ashtar Command, and vibrate with me in my assignment for your planet Earth. I could not fulfill my agreement without you.

You agreed to incarnate to the Earth and when the time was right to unravel from Earthly fear and confusion, to re-align with me and my Command to protect and glide the Earth and its inhabitants through the Ascension doorway.

My assignment as the Commander of the Intergalactic fleets is to lead all galactic Commands and bring us together in harmony to protect the Earth's assignment of Ascension.

I could not do this alone just as you Earthlings cannot do your job alone. We are a collective consciousness from many star systems that have agreed to surround your Earth with our many different light languages. Light languages are color/sound frequencies.

Many of you are now merging with your Galactic brothers and sisters and are actually verbally bringing the languages through you.

These languages are healing your Mother Earth. She is a Master Soul that connects with many other planetary Souls that are already enlightened. As you are verbalizing, singing and bringing these languages through, you are threading the Earth and your collective selves back into the original templates beyond karma.

Many of you are having spontaneous awakenings of light languages coming through you. You are becoming portals of the language that re-connects many others with their planet of origin.

Now, the dilemma is that our shadow brothers and sisters are also slipping reversed programming and frequencies through the languages. Because the light language connections and downloads are new and the different energies coming through are very exciting for you, frequencies that you may not be accustomed to and that are not of the highest light and intention are also slipping through.

Discernment is very, very important here. As your spaceship Earth is gliding through dimensions and you are continuing to expand your energies and awareness, you may have old, karmic energies of the shadow activated in you. If you are not clear emotionally within yourself, the shadow has a karmic portal to come through.

If the language is your highest light, you will feel peace, harmony, love and actually high. If you start feeling confused or doubtful and out of balance, it is a sign of trickster energy interfering with you.

If you feel out of alignment in any way, I strongly advise that you seek assistance from someone who can clear and close the karmic doorway. See all as a gift, even the interference. This gives you the opportunity to clear all levels of your body's frozen emotions and unconsciousness. When you see all as gifts, this moves you into the collective field of love and gratefulness, which actually starts breaking loose and clearing pain body, karmic, lower chakra frequencies.

The shadow's only access in is through fear, ego and unconscious.

All Galactic Commands have come together to protect you and your great Mother Earth through the greatest Souls Awakening you have ever journeyed through.

As I said, you have great assistance. You are not going to lose your planet.

Our Galactic Commands have come together, and we are constantly monitoring and protecting Earth.

I ask that you think of us - thought is energy - and imagine us surrounding your planet with many colors and light languages that are creating a symphony of sound so beautiful that only love and safety can exist.

As you align with us, you become the portals that anchor our mission of love and protection through all dimensions of your world.

As I look at your planet, I see great healings and awakenings. Yes, I also see great chaos. This chaos is the shift of change breaking down old systems so that as a collective consciousness of Souls you can and will re-build a world that is in harmony with all species.

The amazing children being born on your planet now are the future generations of your world. Many of these children are born fully awake. They will re-build your new governments and systems.

When Mother Earth's Soul was brought from Maldek to the Earth, Jeshua, my brother, and I took on the assignment to glide the Earth and all Souls/Cells through the Ascension back home into One consciousness of love.*

Jeshua took on the role as the light carrier of love, to thread the Earth and awaken all of you into One Cell/Soul of love. I agreed to take on the role as the protector of your planet.

Jeshua has a great team of Archangels and Masters that work with him to fulfill this assignment.

I also have a great Galactic team assisting me to protect you and your planet.

You are safe. You are not alone.

Remember, there is no death. The many Beings that have agreed to leave your planet now (some in horrific ways) are actually Beings of light coming home into spirit and opening doorways for you to move through old, emotional, karmic contracts and illusions.

Re-align with the consciousness and light that you want for the world. Become what you want your world to become. You are the world and all consciousness.

You can do this. Move out of fear and into your original agreement and the excitement you felt when you contracted returning to the Earth at this time: the joy, anticipation and excitement of being able to move through and clear all karmic agreements and contracts: the excitement of Co-Creating Heaven on Earth: the excitement of awakening fully into your own inner Master and Co-Creator to merge with all Masters, Angels, and Beings of light to assist the magnificent Earth to glide home safely into the heart of love.

*Read the Creator's chapter explaining Maldek's history in the back of the book.

Thank you for receiving me. Call on me. I am always with you. You will feel me and the safety of my Commands that are surrounding and protecting your world.

I love you, your brother Ashtar.

""I ask that you align with me in my sword of love, of light. Move into my fields and together we will heal your world. We will transform and transmute all fear frequencies to love.""

Message from Archangel Michael

CHAPTER 3

ARCHANGEL MICHAEL'S TRANSMISSION #1

I am here with you now. This is Archangel Michael. We are ONE consciousness. We are ONE world. We are ONE all knowing. I come to you now as you. Fly with me on the wings of love, on the wings of forgiveness, on the wings of compassion for all Beings, not just your light brothers and sisters but also for your shadow brothers and sisters. They are also you. They are also me. What are they mirroring to us that needs to be healed, that needs to be transmuted from fear to love?

Do you not know if you send fear and hatred to them, that you are empowering them? You are feeding them your precious energy. You are diamonds. You are precious gemstones. As you align with their fear frequencies, you are feeding them your beautiful, life force energies of light.

They are taking your light and mirroring yourself back to you through fear. They are mirroring to you many past frequencies of control, manipulation and death, maybe not a physical death but a death of freedom of hope.

The shadows have controlled this world from the beginning of your Earth's history. War and deceit, dishonesty, and fear have ruled for millions of years. Now my beautiful brothers and sisters of light, it is time to disempower the shadow of your world and other worlds by loving them. You don't have to like or agree with what you are seeing and experiencing, but if you align with them in fear, you are collectively vibrating in the morphogenetic fields of fear. This fear breeds more fear.

I ask that you align with me in my sword of love, of light. Move into my fields and together we will heal your world. We will transform and transmute all fear frequencies to love.

The shadow brothers and sisters are hurt children that have become hurt adults.

They empower each other through fear and many have forgotten what they are fighting for.

The karmic history of your planet is coming full circle. The battle between the light and dark or good and evil has always existed on the Earth because the Earth is a karmic planet, a planet where Beings and the collective consciousness awakens out of duality. The only way for that to happen is for duality to be exposed, to come full circle. You are now full circle. The darkness' exposure is from the light awakening multi-dimensionally. The light is activating the shadow multi-dimensionally. This has been by agreement. The dark ones are playing their roles to bring you into the light and you the light carriers have agreed to bring the shadow into the light by freeing yourself karmically. This breaks the collective pattern of duality, of separation.

I know many of you are now experiencing emotions and feelings that go way back through your Soul's history. As you release your own emotions of fear, abandonment, anger, hatred, etc., you release them for the collective because you are the collective. Align with me. Call on me and together we will bring your world into peace, harmony and freedom through love and compassion. Remember we are one consciousness. All that you see is you. As you move into the larger picture of history that is playing out on your planet now, you assist many to move through the doorways and portals back into their birthright of love.

I am always with you. Call on me, and together collectively with all Masters, heavenly Angels, Earth Angels and higher spiritual presences multi-dimensionally, we will hold the love and light of Ascension for all Beings on your planet as well as for your beautiful planet Mother Earth.

Fear breeds fear. Love transmutes fear out of any form.

I am the carrier of the blue flame of protection. Call on me and ask for my flame to wrap itself around you like a blanket of love. With my blue flame around your auric field, you will block any energies that are not of the highest light, or intention. The frequencies will not be able to penetrate my blue shield of love and protection.

The inharmonious frequencies will bounce off of you and dissipate from fear. My blue flame emits a frequency, an energy, which breaks and dissipates all energies that are not of love's light. My assignment is the protection for you and your world's Ascension.

I love you! I AM you.

Archangel Michael

CHAPTER 4

Archangel Michael's Transmission #2

This is Archangel Michael. I come to you as a peace messenger.

All of the turbulence that you see, feel and experience on your planet at this time is the collective shadow in each one of you that has come to the surface to be healed through love, forgiveness and compassion and by moving yourself into the higher realms beyond duality.

Just as you are One consciousness, or frequency, of light multi-dimensionally, you are also many shades of this shadow collectively.

You are experiencing that you are One world, and much of this One world is vibrating in fear.

You are ascending and moving home into the light, or core, of your One Being, the nucleus of the Cell of your Creation.

As you are shifting through the veils of illusion, your inner light collectively has brought all shadow, or unconscious aspects, of your collective selves to the surface to be healed.

Codings of light within your DNA systems are being activated, and you are losing what you thought was your foundation.

It was a temporary earthly foundation. Your real and only foundation is the one of love, of God, of Creation. As you are experiencing and understanding, all other foundations are temporary. They can crumble and be taken from you at any moment.

This election has brought every color, sound and variation of fear that you could experience to the surface to be healed.

Many of you Masters and Lightkeepers on the Earth are very aware of this, and yet the light is also activating all of your old, illusional fear frequencies that needed to be brought to the surface.

As they surface you momentarily align with the collective fear that has awakened.

This fear is the shadow that has been hidden within you and the jowls and grid system of Mother Earth and all civilizations that have inhabited your holographic Earth.

The war is between the light and shadow collectively and multi-dimensionally.

You are ascending, and your earthly civilizations are not so civil now. All emotional memories from lifetimes of separation have been activated, all the way back to the original split from Source, from the One Cell of Creation from which you were all created.

The upheaval on your planet now is not an accident. It has affected your whole world because you are the whole world.

You, as a collective, have agreed that at this time of your Souls' history and awakening, you will take your power back from all entities, organizations and religions that have controlled you, which have taken your light and life-force to empower themselves.

The false reign of power is coming to an end. You have agreed to allow this illusional foundation to surface and collapse. From this DNA activation of Ascension, you will shift the illusional power out of fearful frequencies and into the real power, which is the Source of Creation, of Love, of God, of You!

When you truly understand that this is by agreement, you will shift and move out of fear and connect to the light at the end of this "Dark Night of the Soul."

And there is a light! You are the Light! I ask that you collectively come together in the higher agreement and download the frequency of love, light, peace, harmony and equality for all people.

The two candidates in your U.S. election are of the same Soul group and vibration. In the higher dimension, they are on the same side. They are from the Master Soul that agreed to split from the lower chakras' colors into fear, conflict and confusion.

Their agreement was to come to the Earth to activate the split between the male and female, the heart and Ego, the light and shadow, and your collective agreement is to heal the split.

If they were not great Masters, they would not have the power to bring you and your World together in the great division of so many emotional stories.

As you look at the election, every karmic agreement and emotional story that a Soul individually and collectively has been through was brought to the surface: dishonesty, greed, sexual violation abuse, prejudice, fear, ego and many more divisions.

The only way to heal and transmute these fear-based illusions is for them to surface so that you can choose which ideals you want in your life and for the collective.

Many of those who are protesting did not actually vote. They put their blinders on thinking that all would go away, and when the outcome was not in their favor, their fear and injustice came to the surface.

They gave their power away to fear and closed their eyes. As you look at your own lives, you may see that you have allowed this same pattern to disempower you.

You are the light at the end of the tunnel! You are the highest Source power of love, of light, of the higher consciousness of the collective pattern playing itself out on your planet now.

Empower yourself and the world by coming together in gratefulness of all old emotions coming to the surface to be healed. Honor the fact that you are on the Earth at this time when you have the choice and ability to choose what you want for yourself and the world. Transmute the collective fear frequencies into love by collectively vibrating in the higher knowledge, purpose and picture of the Ascension.

Call on me and all of the Angels and Masters that are holding the light for this incredible collective Souls Awakening.

This is the Ascension! You are ascending, and together we have agreed to become the wings of love that will shift your planet and all inhabitants back home into One Cell/Soul of love, of Creation.

You are the Masters that have gone before. Be and become what you want your world to become. Think what you want your world to be. Thought is energy and power. Match and merge into the light of freedom for all.

You absolutely are not losing your planet. You are awakening and shifting into the higher heart of love and into freedom. Think, feel and see freedom, and it shall be.

Know that all is divinely planned and agreed upon, and just as your candidates had a great Master plan to assist in the awakening of the shadow of duality, you, as Masters and Co-Creators have agreed to merge together with us to shift your world into love, peace, harmony, justice and freedom for all.

Call on me. Align and become One with me and all other Masters and Angels of light whose assignment is to assist you and Mother Earth through all Ascension activations and portals home into One Soul, One heart of love, of Creation.

I love you. I am you!

Archangel Michael

CHAPTER 5

ARCHANGEL MICHAEL'S TRANSMISSION #3

This is Archangel Michael. I come to you now to re-assure you that all is well, and you are safe. The divine plan of your world's Ascension is playing out exactly as planned.

The Earth is a very special commodity. She is the only holographic planet where Beings such as yourselves have the opportunity to awaken, experience and to clear out all karmic, emotional patterns.

Just as you individually have come full circle, meaning: every emotional experience, both hurtful and loving, in this lifetime has a frame of reference elsewhere. This is the lifetime of karmic completion for yourself and the collective.

Every civilization that has ever lived on the Earth is also coming full circle to heal and clear all collective, karmic debts and deaths.

This does not mean you will not re-incarnate to the Earth again; it means that every person, situation and experience you are going through you have been through before. You have agreed to come to the Earth to understand, forgive, heal and clear the old, emotional hurts and bondages.

You are the collective consciousness of the old patterns and also civilizations. You are the Atlanteans, the Lemurians, the Egyptians, the Mayans, and all other civilizations that have ever inhabited your planet. Many of you are also from Maldek, the planet from which Mother Earth's Soul was originally birthed. After Maldeks death, Mother Earths Soul was then brought to the Earth. You collectively are in the death, or end times, of these civilizations. Many of these civilizations died, or came to an end, from the ego shadow warring against each other.

They came to an end of their learning experience, or agreements.

Now, you light Beings on the Earth have lived in and experienced many deaths of these civilizations. Just as you individually have come to the Earth to clear out old, karmic, emotional stories and agreements, you collectively are clearing out the end times of these civilizations.

The collective memories and emotions of the demise and death of these civilizations have erupted like volcanoes.

Your agreement is to move into the higher light and purpose of the emotional eruptions and align with us, the Masters of light to lift and shift your world through the Ascension and into the re-birth: the birth of One nation with God and liberty, justice, equality and freedom for all.

I am here to re-assure you that you are not going to lose your beautiful Mother Earth, and you are not losing your earthly civilizations. The old fear-based unconsciousness of many of these cultures is breaking loose.

You are shifting out of duality, out of separation, out of prejudice and fear, and you will merge together with us in love and harmony.

You cannot do this without us, and we cannot do this without you. We are on the same team and have the same assignment: to be the wings of love, light and highest intention for Mother Earth and all of you, her inhabitants, to shift multi-dimensionally and glide through all Ascension portals into the re-birth of our heart and One love.

The Earth is a hologram, and all end times are playing out at the same time. Because each civilization had its own frequency and purpose, the Earth has many different energies and consciousnesses that are waking up and fighting for life or the re-birth and breath of God.

You are becoming ONE world in this great awakening and re-birth.

You are shifting and clearing the end times of all karmic agreements individually and of all collective civilizations.

The only way this can happen is for the emotional, karmic patterns to re-surface, which they are doing now.

As you heal these patterns within yourselves, you are healing and shifting for the collective because you are the collective.

I ask that you move out of fear of the pain body that has erupted on your planet and into the higher dimensions of yourselves, of the higher intention of this re-birth.

Stay connected to your higher self, to our higher selves, to the higher self of Mother Earth (Gaia), and align your thoughts and emotions to the mind and heart of God, of Creation, so that we can collectively birth you and your beautiful planet into the realms of Heaven on Earth.

You are not alone. You are safe. We are constantly with you monitoring the emotions of the amazing re-birth of your New World.

Call on me – on us – and we will lift you into the safety of the higher knowing and purpose of your great Souls Awakening.

Fear is the collective, karmic emotions erupting. Love is the safety of the re-birth through the pain body's emotions.

You are awakening into the Masters and Co-Creators within yourself. The veils are lifting, and from this awakening, you have the choice as to what and where you choose to align your energy.

Thank you for receiving me. I love you. I am you.

Archangel Michael

CHAPTER 6

Light Walkers Among Us

We walk on the Earth to open the dimensions.

We walk between dimensions on the Earth to shift in the awakening consciousness of your world.

We come from many planetary systems to assist the shift of Earth into higher vibrations so she can become one Soul/Cell consciousness with other planetary Soul systems.

Just as you on Earth are from many planets, universes and Creations, so are we.

You Earthlings are now blending together beyond race, gender, creed, religions, and belief systems.

It seems like your Earth is in great turmoil, which it is, but it is not so seemingly out of balance. It is waking up as you, the collective consciousness, on the Earth is also waking up.

Together you are going through great growing pains as the walls of separation are being exposed and broken down. The systems of the Earth are all breaking down, which must happen so new systems can be put in place. The new cannot be put on top of the old.

Some of your Earthly systems are ancient. They were needed at the time because they matched and mirrored the level of consciousness, or awareness, that the many different star systems, Beings of light, that had incarnated to your planet needed. The system threaded people together in their own chosen environment meaning each country, civilization, and culture had their agreed upon karma to play out.

As you and the Earth are ascending together and coming back together as one people, or Soul consciousness, all of these seemingly secure systems are breaking down, which is the higher agreement on all levels.

The chaos in your world is collective karma breaking loose and the emotions coming out sideways and all over the place.

We are one consciousness. All that you see is you. Both of the candidates that were seeking the presidency in the United States are you. When you understand this, which one of yourselves do you want to bash, discredit and put down?

Perhaps the road to take would be the one of holding the mirror of love and light for both of yourselves to awaken and be the best that you can be, to serve the people in the highest consciousness of good for all people and all countries.

When you really understand this, why would you want to send fear, loathing, hatred and worthlessness to yourself?

Haven't you already experienced enough of that within yourself? Hasn't that been what you have wanted to bring yourself out of in this lifetime?

You are incredible, amazing Beings of light, Masters of light and love that have agreed to come to the Earth, lower your consciousness, and as you wake up and remember who you are, bring the collective back into the light. You are the light of the world. Choose wisely which energy you want to align with, which frequency you desire to project back to yourself. Whatever the question, love is always the answer.

Remember if you can feel it, you can heal it.

The way to change the world, the consciousness, is to change yourself to become what you want the world to be. Call on us and consciously match and merge with our highest intentions for you and your world. Together we can and will shift your world into Heaven on Earth.

CHAPTER 7

LEMURIANS SPEAKING – LOVE'S AWAKENING

Once upon a time in a land far away was a consciousness of Lemuria. It was a civilization of Beings from many planets and Creations. These Beings of light agreed to come to this planet called Earth to seed it with the consciousness of Love. The Beings that settled in Lemuria were from many planets, galaxies and universes that were already enlightened.

Now many of you inhabiting the Earth are aspects of Lemurian Beings. Many of you come from the Co-Creation of the Lemurian seeds.

Just as many different races, religions, and belief systems are coming together and Co-Creating on the Earth now, the same experience happened on Lemuria. The difference is that the Lemurians were already enlightened Beings. They were not necessarily ascended Beings, but they were enlightened.

When they brought children into the world, they planted seeds for future generations that would inhabit the Earth. Some of these future Beings are you that are threading back through time and remembering your Lemurian roots. Not only are you remembering your roots – the origination of your Creation – but you are activating the grid systems, or roots, of Mother Earth to awaken her into the frequencies of love, compassion and Oneness. These frequencies are creating what seems to be havoc on your Earth and in the Earth's atmosphere.

This is because your higher love frequencies are merging with all energies of war, hatred, fear, and ego that have played out on the Earth since the beginning of the Earth's journey of karmic clearing.

As I said, Lemurians were enlightened, but many had not ascended. You Lemurians are carrying the DNA of your ancestor Lemurians that planted the love seed of Oneness for the Earth.

You are the future generations of Lemurian seeds that carry the original blueprint of Lemurian's love agreement.

You are ascending along with your planet, and all of the dimensions that Lemurian Beings of love had not ascended into are now activating.

As you and the Earth are ascending, all of the ancestral Lemurian strands in your DNA that were not vibrating in the original love template have now awakened.

And you, the future generations of Lemuria, are experiencing much duality and separation within yourselves. Your ancestors' original love template has been activated. As you are awakening into your inner knowing of your highest God/Goddess source self, this empowerment of love and the original template of love are merging together through all dimensions of you.

This is creating combustions of fear, confusion, emptiness, loneliness, of not belonging, of death and most of all of re-birth. Because there really is no death, a Soul never dies. As it leaves the Earth, it transmutes karmic energies into knowingness for itself and all ancestral Beings connected to the Soul.

The death/re-birth has a rippling effect through all of humanity starting with the closest biological family from this lifetime and then through karmic relationships in the DNA.

You seedlings are here to Co-Create Heaven on Earth, to

become open portals of light that other Souls will merge into. You are merging back into One Soul/Cell self of Creation before time.

Your planet Earth is a planet of karmic completion. All that you see on the Earth now are Souls waking up through all dimensions of themselves.

The light within has become so bright that it is activating your inner shadow selves through all dimensions.

The same is happening collectively as your collective light is hitting the morphogenetic fields that are still vibrating in fear. Combustions are happening and the Cells, Souls of your planet, are acting out in sickness, dis-ease and fear.

Many of you are having mental, emotional, and physical health problems. The same is happening collectively. If you could imagine the whole collective consciousness as one large body of Creation, you would see how the light in this collective consciousness body is activating old, karmic energies of fear.

Your physical bodies are Cells of this larger, multi-dimensional consciousness. Just as your physical bodies are clearing your entire karmic ancestral history, the same is happening for the collective consciousness of the world.

As you heal and clear your own bodies karmically, you are doing it for the world because you are the world.

Cells interact and communicate with each other. What message do you want to send to your Cells? What frequency do you want to vibrate in collectively? Which morphogenetic field do you choose to support? Your whole journey in this lifetime is to return to your beginning roots, DNA system of love.

It all begins within. You are the Masters, Co-Creators, the Lemurian seedlings, awakening through all dimensions of yourself through the beginning history. You are moving through your Soul's seemly separation from the one Soul/Cell consciousness and back home into One love.

You are now coming home, individually and collectively. You are returning to the source of love within yourself. Your self-love has a domino effect as it turns the love switch on for the collective.

You are the Wayshowers, the Lemurians, coming full circle and guiding the whole collective Soul/Cell consciousness through many portals of light. The light portals are activating the memories and knowing of love.

See the world and yourself full of love and healing, and you will move into the morphogenetic field's multi-dimensions of love. Many of you are now merging into higher dimensions of yourself. Your higher dimensional selves are actually guiding you home inside of yourself and into the nucleus of One Cell consciousness of God/Creation – love. Welcome home beloved ones.

CHAPTER 8

JESHUA

This is Jeshua. I come to you as Your brother, Your sister, Your mother, Your father, Your child. I come to you as You, for all that you experience is Me: My light is activating and holding the love for you to awaken into the magnificent child of God's love in which you were first created.

We are not separate. I am not outside of you to worship. I am you.

I come from the same thread of existence, of Creation, that you come from. We are one energy that has split out of one cell to Co-Create an experience of love throughout all time frames.

I am you. Now is the time that you My brother and sister have agreed to come back home inside of yourself.

I am the light within you that is activating your own flow of love. I went before and opened the memories and portals of love for you to go through.

I am in your DNA because I am you. You are Me. As We are ascending together and you are moving through many dimensions collectively; coding of the Christ consciousness in your DNA is now being activated. This consciousness is love: love and forgiveness for all that you see - love and forgiveness for all that you don't see or understand.

The only way to heal and shift your world out of the fear duality on your planet is through love, forgiveness and compassion.

You don't have to understand to forgive. From the third dimensional consciousness, you won't understand the larger picture of your world's history that is unraveling and playing out.

I know first-hand that the Ascension process of death and rebirth is not easy. Many years ago on your Earth, I agreed to go through the Ascension to open a portal for you, the collective, to be able to transcend time, move out of duality and back into One heart of love.

I went through a painful death, and in the middle of the suffering I momentarily forgot My higher mission and purpose. I also felt that God had forsaken Me.

In the moment of pain and suffering, I had connected to the pain, fear, conflict and confusion of your world's experience and perception of God/Creation. I had moved into the morphogenetic field of fear, of the collective pain body's frequencies.

I needed that experience. I needed to know first-hand how a person in fear and pain can forget the larger picture of their Soul's experience and feel rejected and forgotten by Our Father/Mother God.

How could I have compassion and understanding for you had I not experienced your emotional journey?

As I said, I went before and opened the Ascension door for you collectively to move through. I was not alone; I had many Masters and Angels around Me holding the light, love and higher frequency for Me to move through.

You are not alone; you also have many Masters and Angels around you. They are actually threading and blending their energies with you as you move through and clear karmic cycles and energies through all of the time lines that your Soul has agreed to experience.

As you look at your world, you may have a sense of hopelessness and despair.

The greed, fear and collective ego is very much exposed.

This is the lifetime that you have agreed to come full circle individually and collectively. All that you see is old, karmic aspects of duality that have come to the surface and are playing themselves out collectively.

It appears that the shadow, or darkness, has put a gloom of fear on your planet.

Actually the multi-dimensional light has become so high and bright that it is activating old, karmic lineage of the shadow, or darkness.

This is the shadow that was hiding, or looming, behind the scenes or curtains.

The light has brought the old control and secrets to the surface. The old systems of fear and control are breaking loose and doing what they can to not lose control.

They have no power on their own; they live off of your fear. They control you through fear and you then feed the collective fear energy your light, which empowers them.

Your planet Earth is a planet of karmic completion. There have been many civilizations that have collectively played out their karmic agreements and transitioned back into spirit.

The roots, or major patterns, that the civilizations carried are now clearing themselves out through hurricanes, tornados, earthquakes.

The old, karmic emotions that the grid system the Mother Earth was carrying are emptying.

This is the Ascension. Mother Earth is ascending with you.

You are the Cells of Mother Earth. You are both going through the same process. The Ascension light is activating your old emotions of fear, guilt, shame, hopelessness, conflict, confusion, worthlessness and many more frozen emotions that are erupting. Many of you are losing your sense of self, of who you thought you were. This is forcing you to surrender and let go.

It is not a comfortable place in which to vibrate. As you surrender and the old, emotional stories start breaking loose and clearing, you are ascending into the memories of your light, of who you are in the higher dimensions of yourself.

They (old emotions) must come to the surface to clear them. The same thing is happening to the collective consciousness of your world and to Mother Earth.

This is what you see playing out on your planet. It may seem like your world is in a "Dark Night of the Soul." There is a light at the end of the tunnel. As you look at your own life's journey, there were probably experiences that felt like a "dark night." As you shifted through the darkness and back into the light, your whole perception of life started changing.

The same is happening collectively. It may appear to become darker before you merge fully through the unconsciousness back into a great understanding of your real power of love. So many songs, stories, movies, etc. are now being written and created about love.

You are becoming conscious as to what is really important: Joy, happiness, forgiveness, freedom, gratitude, Oneness; everything is happening for a reason. These words and phrases are what are commonly being spoken of.

Your DNA system is awakening and merging into My Christ DNA system of love.

We are becoming one DNA system of many beautiful, blended, golden strands of Creation.

As I ascended and opened a portal for you to move through,

you are now ascending, becoming one with Me, and the portal is expanding itself through all time lines of Creation and into Oneness.

You are Co-Creating a new world, a world where the feminine is now empowered, loved and supported to continue to expand the frequencies of love through all of Creation.

The feminine is the heart of love: your spiritual home and awakening.

We are coming home together with both the male and female inside of ourselves. Our collective feminine is aligning with the morphogenetic fields of the power of love.

This love is opening our hearts to honor the feminine of your world.

We have all lived many lives and have so many identities that are playing out within us. As I said we have all been male and female. This is why there is seemingly so much gender confusion on your planet now.

The confusion is: Souls are awakening into their genetic makeup beyond this world.

The gift is allowing people to become who they truly feel they are on so many levels and for the collective consciousness to accept each other regardless of what body or role you choose to live in.

Imagine physically playing out both roles in one lifetime. This is very challenging and at the same time very freeing: having the opportunity to experience and live out both genders in one lifetime is very freeing. This clears out karmic agreements in the DNA of the separation between the male and female.

I speak to you of this because even the male has great feminine qualities and feelings. As your earthly consciousness is evolving, the male is now allowing himself to come into balance with his own feminine and his heart is opening and surrendering into the safety of love.

Even if he is not changing the physical body, he is coming to the balance of the male and female within. The same is happening for the feminine; she is safe to fully open her heart and allow her love and sensitivity to be her empowering guiding light.

As she becomes safe to guide through the strength of her heart, her inner male will support her feminine to go forward to change the world's consciousness beyond what she could ever imagine.

As you love, accept, and balance your own inner feminine and male, you align with the balance of Mother/Father Creator, the balance of Magdalene and My love, the balance of all of the Archangels and Masters. You become one with the ebb and flow of Creation. You don't have to think about the next step in your life. You are in the flow and knowingness of your Soul's higher purpose and journey.

This is what you call surrendering and allowing the balance within to come home into the freedom of your Soul, to move into your Soul's song, and become the nucleus of the One Cell in which you were first created.

Magdalene is my feminine. We are one Soul that split and came to the Earth to balance the male and female. I could not have gone through My death and re-birth (Ascension) without Her love creating a safety net for Me to move through My Soul's agreement. She is Me in a different body, My twin flame.

Even though We both knew My journey and what was to come, the emotional responsibility and separation was very challenging for both of Us. We felt the same feelings of loss, separation and grief that many of you on the Earth are feeling.

Magdalene balanced Me and I balanced Her. We were one Soul holding the love and light for each other on Our Soul's Awakening journey.

We went before and opened the twin flame frequency for many of you to merge into now.

As you are shifting and awakening multi-dimensionally, many of you are awakening and meeting twin aspects of yourself on the Earth plane. Many of these aspects may be the same gender as you.

All Souls have both components of the male and female. You are igniting each other's flame regardless of what gender you are physically living in now.

I know first-hand that awakening into ascended Masters and Co-Creators on the Earth is not easy and yet the gift of coming full circle and blending yourself, your Soul's song, with the other Masters that have gone before you is a glorious homecoming of love that is beyond any Earthly perception.

As you continue to awaken through so many dimensions of yourself, you will glide back into the heart of love with your beloved twin flame.

Your flame may not physically be on the Earth at this time, but because there is no time or distance, your divine aspect of love will connect with your heart and you will have a sense of completion and wholeness within yourself. Your twin will be one of your guiding lights. You will become One mind and heart, One consciousness.

This is the Ascension. We are multi-dimensional beings and are now re-connecting and aligning ourselves with all aspects of our Soul.

Magdalene and I are the overseers of your planet. Our

balanced energy of love, of the Christ consciousness, is activating codings of the Christ within you, and We are awakening and becoming One Christ.

Call on Me, on Us. We are not outside of you. I am you. We are with you. Together We will glide your planet home into freedom. I love you. We love you.

Jeshua and Magdalene

CHAPTER 9

MAGDALENE SPEAKS

My journey to awaken the feminine on your Earth may seem lengthy to many of you, but in spirit there is no time or distance. This journey for me has been and is a blink of the eye through all time frequencies. It has always been as I have always been.

I am so honored to be of service to be the feminine Christ that is leading you through the portal beyond duality and separation and into the heart of love, of sacred union.

Jeshua's journey on the Earth was karmic. He went through a death and re-birth to show you that life is eternal, that there truly is no death, only a shifting of vibrations from fear and confusion and into One Soul/Cell of love. I was on the Earth with him and was his anchor to assist him to remember his origin of love. He had me to vibrate with him in our Parents/Mother-Father/God's love. I held the frequency for him to go through the karmic death, to open the portal of Ascension for all to move through.

The Ascension portal was an opening of light that spread from the Heavens and into the Earth and you, the inhabitants or Cells of the Earth.

The light activated the grid system of your great Mother Earth. This was by agreement. The Earth has gone through many cycles of death and re-birth of many civilizations collectively playing out all karmic emotions.

You have had many higher conscious civilizations that were quite barbaric, that were vibrating in duality.

Jeshua's and my agreement for your Earth was and is to move you out of duality.

As he ascended through the death of karma, he opened the door for all to move through the portal. As the heavenly light spread into the grid of the Earth, it actually started awakening you who are walking the Earth's journey.

Mother Earth is sacred, and I watch and experience many of you honoring her and loving her. Her role is even greater than what you have understood.

Not only has her grid system been filled with duality of civilizations, her grid system also holds the highest love, light, and consciousness of Creation. When Jeshua ascended, the light of freedom, of the Heavens, of all Masters and Angels that have gone before and all future consciousness of Oneness was downloaded into her.

As you walk the Earth, her vibrations are actually awakening you into the Masters within yourself.

Through her seasons of winter, spring, summer and fall, she is constantly shifting and clearing out the old and making room for the higher vibrations that she is already holding. Because she is ascending and the Ascension portals are wide open, she is vibrating through you collectively and activating your DNA to clear old, karmic civilizations that you are still vibrating in. She is activating the light civilizations and also the unconscious civilizations of duality that are within you.

The activation is bringing up all of your old, fear frequencies as well as your light frequencies. The light is activating all within you that no longer serves your Soul in the highest.

For many this is breaking out in sickness and dis-ease. This dis-ease is not from just this lifetime. The dis-ease moves through all cycles of your Soul's journey, and the old, fear emotions are breaking down, clearing out, creating sickness and dis-ease.

This is happening collectively and is why so many people are vibrating in the same sickness.

What an incredible opportunity to be on the Earth at this time, to clear and clean out old systems individually and collectively, to awaken into your future selves in your physical body.

You don't have to wait until you leave your physical bodies to come home into love, to awaken into your full bloom of Spirit.

You are moving through all veils, Co-Creating Heaven on Earth.

As Mother Earth is ascending beyond time and into her future self that is already ascended, she is very powerfully clearing old ego, fear-based, karmic emotions that have been vibrating in her grid system.

This is forcing you, the Souls of the Earth, to let go of much of your materialism, control, ego, etc. and bringing you to your knees in surrender and hopelessness.

Many of you are on your knees praying for help and assistance. We hear you; we are with you; you are not alone. We are answering your prayers, just maybe not in the ways you think they should be answered.

We are answering your prayers in love, opening your hearts to be grateful for life, opening your hearts to love, to assist one another, opening your hearts beyond color, gender, religion, political beliefs, etc.

We are opening your hearts to become One world of love, support and freedom for all.

Mother Earth is a Master Soul. She is very conscious of her agreement at this time. She is a very powerful feminine consciousness that is healing the feminine of your world.

My agreement is to also awaken and heal the feminine in your world - not just the feminine in the female but also awaken the safety of the feminine love in the male of your world.

You see many old roles, or systems, between the female and male breaking down. You are moving out of gender roles and back into a system of equality.

The hierarchies of your higher dimensions and worlds are blending with your worlds, and we are all coming together in balance of the male and female throughout all of Creation.

Mother Earth could not do her assignment alone. She also has her beloved Father Earth. When the 2012 doorway opened, she merged back into his arms of love.

He is not in physical form. He is an energy, or etheric Earth of male frequency, that has integrated with Mother Earth. He is giving her the balance and strength to move us all into the new world.

Jeshua would have had a more difficult time with his Earthly journey had I, the feminine, not been there to hold his heart in mine to give him the strength of love to persevere.

Yes, he had our Mother/Father's love, and on the Earth plane it was important to have the feminine love and safety for him to remember his own origin of love.

Now, on your Earth at this time, it is the feminine that is shifting you out of duality, out of survival, out of the unconscious, out of fear and back into One heart of love.

Jeshua is holding the love, light and safety for me merging in full bloom of my feminine love and power to assist you to awaken into, bloom into, the memories of your Soul's love, your birthright of love, the love in which you were first created.

Jeshua and I are One consciousness. We flow in and out of each other. We are the balance and truth of love that is awakening the greatest memories of love in all of you.

You are awakening into the teaching of love, forgiveness and compassion that Jeshua brought to your Earth. As your DNA is being activated into your Christ consciousness, you are becoming the teaching of love.

Your agreement of awakening love is aligning with Mother Earth's grid system of love and is shifting your world into your new world consciousness.

I, Magdalene, and your beautiful Mother Earth are working heart to heart to shift your world through all portals of light into One Soul/Cell love consciousness of Creation.

We both have our beloved male aspects of the Christ: I with Jeshua and Mother Earth with her beloved protector Father Earth.

Because you are us, the Cells of us, you also are moving into the flow of the male and female, yin and yang, within yourselves. All that is not the balance is being activated to cleanse and clear you individually and collectively into the balance and ebb and flow of Creation.

Call on me, Magdalene – the feminine Christ, your Mother of the Christ consciousness of love. You will feel me with you. I will answer your call. I love you. I AM you. I am greatly honored to have the role of the feminine Christ for your world.

Magdalene

*Read Jeshua's and Magdalene's Love Story (earthly re-union) in the back of the book.

*"I carry the flame of wisdom to assist you
to merge from the caterpillar and into
the beautiful butterfly of freedom.
Allow my wings of love to gracefully
fly with you home into the light,
heart and consciousness of God"*

Message from Archangel Uriel

CHAPTER 10

Archangel Uriel Speaks

I am with you now. This is Uriel. I am the peacemaker between Heaven and Earth.

I am the direct link between my heart and yours to the heart of the Creator.

When I speak of the Creator, I am speaking of the balanced male/female, heart-soul-mind of the infinite Soul Spirit of Creation.

I am speaking of the energy source of your Creation. Just like all of you have a divine purpose for your Soul's journey on the Earth, all Archangels and Masters have our assignment for the Earth's Ascension and evolution.

Yes, I am speaking of evolution. As you, the human species, continue to evolve mentally, emotionally and physically, the same is happening for your beautiful planet Earth.

Much of what you see as catastrophic is the Earth clearing her throat and shedding old layers of collective, karmic skin. She is ascending and awakening into her higher self and Oversoul. Her Oversoul is aligning with other planets and Oversouls that have already ascended home.

You are coming together collectively and holding the light for one another to remember that you are magnificent Beings of light - that you are so much more than your earthly self could ever imagine. Mother Earth has many star systems and planets that are also holding the light in her transition of merging into One Soul with them.

Together they are gliding us home through all star systems, galaxies and dimensions. Imagine being on a beautiful, alive starship and together we are gliding through all consciousness and unconsciousness. As we are gliding through many time portals, we, with Mother Earth, are also holding the light for other planets and systems to awaken.

Everything is energy and has a consciousness. Just as you have agreed to lower your understanding and come to the Earth to awaken, the same has been true for collective civilizations that live, or reside, on other planets.

DNA codings throughout your whole galaxies and universes are being activated, and you are expanding multi-dimensionally into other universes and galaxies.

As above, so below or below is also the same as above. All of Creation and consciousness is evolving. This is the evolution. It could not be any other way. This is the ebb and flow of consciousness, or Creation. All is constant movement and change.

Just as your Earth is always moving around the sun, the Cells of your Souls are constantly moving and shedding all old, worn-out frequencies and awakening into the new, evolved you. Evolution is amazing. Nothing ever sits still. All is constant movement.

Now what do I, Uriel, have to do with the collective evolution of Creation? I, with other Archangels and Masters, are constantly monitoring the frequencies of the shift of change.

I, the Soul of Uriel, exist through all time lines and dimensions as you do. My beginning is the nucleus of the Master Cell of Creation. From my beginning I am able to hold and vibrate frequencies for all of you to expand and awaken into the memory of your own inner knowing and wisdom.

This is my mission and purpose. My frequency is the direct link into the heart of you, of the heart of the One Cell/Soul that we all expanded from.

Imagine your body's Cells as they continue to split and expand. Along the way they may find or experience a Cell that seems to be contaminated with an old virus, or old belief system of fear. The contaminated Cell will do its best to befriend the light, or healthy Cell, to pull it close and use its light to be able to exist or stay alive.

The contaminated Cell is aligned collectively with a fear-based frequency of sound that continues to feed it or keep it alive. The fear is old, karmic emotions that thread back through your Soul's collective history and into the original split from Source.

The illusion of the original split from Source created a great misalignment from the one original Cell, or Soul blueprint of Creation.

The misalignment broke the sound barrier of the original Soul/Cell of love fragmenting and creating imaginary fear, mistrust and abandonment by God, or Source. Because you are from the original Cell of God, your physical body's Cells are also carrying the imprint of the emotional impact of the separation.

This has created Cells that vibrate in fear. Any of your Cells that are vibrating in sickness, or dis-ease, are missing the original template of the color/sound frequency of love in which you were first created. They are the fragmented aspects, or Cells, that aligned with each other in fear.

So my job is to assist you, the Cell/Souls of the Master

Cell of Creation to experience the memories of love, of your Soul's highest Creation.

All of the misalignment, imbalance and disharmony that is playing itself out in your physical bodies as dis-ease can be followed back to the original illusional, emotional split from Source. There is no exception to this!

Your bodies are full of Cells that are constantly vibrating and communicating with each other. Your physical body is also a big Cell of a larger body, or consciousness. This larger body, or Cell, is your Soul group that you incarnated to the Earth with. Your Soul group vibrates together with a larger Cell consciousness. You and your Soul group's Cells are constantly communicating with each other. Each Soul/Cell group has its larger intentions for your world.

Your collective Cell consciousness is communicating with the expanded Cell/Soul group beyond your Earthly Cell/Soul group.

Your Cells are constantly communicating with Cells/Souls of your collective Soul's groups through all dimensions and back into one Cell/Soul group of Creation. This is the oneness that so many of you have awakened into the memory of. The Master Cell/Soul that I, Uriel, vibrate in is unconditional love and acceptance. I vibrate through all time lines and Soul groups to clear Cells of fear, to transmute fear Cells into the original template of love.

The seeming challenge for many of you is to shift through the old, multi-dimensional emotions of fear. There is no need to continue to vibrate in fear.

You are the collective consciousness of all emotions, from all lifetimes that you have ever lived through. This is the lifetime that you have agreed to come full circle. Every emotional experience that you have ever traveled through has a frame of reference elsewhere. Meaning this is the lifetime of cleaning out these old memories. When you can find the pattern within you from the other lifetime, you can clear it instantly.

You have had many lifetimes where you lived in constant joy, love, happiness, and freedom: lifetimes of enlightenment; lifetimes as great Masters, Teachers and Wayshowers; lifetimes in spirit as spirit guides and teachers. You are vast libraries of knowledge and wisdom. You are not victims. You agreed to incarnate into this lifetime to clear old, collective, karmic emotions of fear to awaken, bring forth and merge with the incredible knowledge and wisdom that you carry within.

Some of you are from the first wave of the original split from Source. You carry within you the original fragmented aspects of fear and abandonment.

As you incarnated you passed the fearful emotions through your whole genetic time line. Your DNA system threaded the future generations birthed after you with the missing frequency, or tone. The re-activation and re-alignment of this tone will thread you into wholeness. This was passed down through all generations of your Soul and into your parents in this lifetime. You agreed for them to pass the fear frequencies into you to come full circle. As the light bearer in your karmic genetic DNA systems, you can clear and clean the patterns out for yourself and your family. This clearing shifts through time and back into the original pattern of separation.

This is why you are experiencing so much sickness and dis-ease in you, the Souls, awakening on your planet now. This dis-ease is a collective consciousness that threads all the way back into the original split. You who are carrying the splits emotions are short-circuiting and your Cells are awakening into the sound of fear and abandonment. The frequency was already in your Cells and was re-activated in this lifetime of clearing and completion.

The original split was not an accident. As a collective Soul/Cell, you all agreed to awaken into more knowing states of consciousness. Many of you agreed to become fragmented and move into the experience and expression of duality.

The Souls/Cells that did not fragment agreed to hold the light for your Soul's journey. As you ventured into many feelings and emotions of separation, you fed these emotions back to the light holders so they would understand people's emotional stories. Some of the light holders are great Spirit Guides, Angels, Masters and Teachers in many dimensions that have not actually been on the Earth or on other karmic planets or experiences.

They understand emotions and how to guide and assist others through their karmic, emotional agreements from you.

You were great Teachers for them, and now full circle, they are great guides and Teachers for you. They are bringing you back home through the karmic portals into love, light, harmony and grace.

You have done this, come full circle together: Always students and teachers - teachers and students.

As you come back home within, you are awakening and remembering that you are the Master Teachers and Angels that have been guiding you. You are the ones that have gone before you.

You are remembering that higher aspects of yourself have

been channeling and guiding you home and are now integrating with you.

Now, back to the sickness, dis-ease, and separation that your Cells may be communicating with and attaching to other Cells.

You are multi-dimensional Beings of light that vibrate through many dimensions and morphogenetic fields. When you understand this, you can dis-connect from the collective fields (morphogenetic fields) of sickness and dis-ease and through constant intention move into the collective fields and Cells' communication of love, health, safety, wholeness, freedom and Oneness.

At first this frightens your dis-eased Cells and they do everything that they can to not die off. They will actually send vapors of fear throughout your bodies and connect to old, fear-based emotions to stay alive. This will throw you back into fear of survival and send the color and sound of death through all of your bodies and systems. The dis-eased Cells then feel fed and powerful and will attack and choke the healthy Cells into surrendering.

Your mind, thought, feelings and emotions affect all of your Cells and bodies. Unless your agreement in this lifetime is to download the collective dis-ease and become the portal of light to transmute the sickness fear into love by leaving the Earth, you have the highest possibility ever to heal yourself.

You cannot do this alone. All Cells are collective, and as you move into the highest collective consciousness of love's safety, you will allow love to transmute your Cells' fear into health, vitality and wholeness. Love will dissipate fear into love, and the dis-ease will clear from your bodies and systems.

This is why you see and experience so many miraculous

healings taking place in many. They move through all timelines instantly and awaken into love.

Call on me. I am of service to you and your world. My sword of light extends from the heart, Soul and nucleus of our One Creation.

I carry the flame of wisdom to assist you to merge from the caterpillar and into the beautiful butterfly of freedom. Allow my wings of love to gracefully fly with you home into the light, heart and consciousness of God, of Creation.

I love you. I AM you.

Archangel Uriel

CHAPTER 11

THE CREATOR SPEAKS
OUR COLLECTIVE SOULS AWAKENING

"Love is beyond duality or separation - Love is!"

You are now on a cellular level remembering who you are. You are awakening into the magnificent light crystal Beings of your Soul's highest Creation. You are awakening and moving collectively out of old belief systems, prejudices, separations, conflicts, dualities and illusions.

It is the intention now for all of Creation to bloom and expand into its highest expression of knowing. It is only then that all can vibrate in balance and harmony and full bloom of love.

Because the world is now in such extremes, you get to see clearly, or have mirrored back to you, your own perceptions of reality. If you experience anything as negative, fearful, or incomplete, it is because this is the way you are still experiencing yourself. You cannot change anyone or anything else; the uncluttering must be within yourself. The change, or healing, must start within you. As you love and accept all aspects of yourself, including your ego Shadow, you can love and accept all aspects of others on their Souls' journey.

When your emotions and mind balance each other and support each other in love, harmony, and integrity, a balance of all consciousness realigns itself with you. You then see everyone, every player, in the divine perfection of your own magnificence, harmony, and Oneness. You will feel everyone, everything, every player in his/her own experience, as perfection and the divine consciousness of love.

As you start to experience life through your higher heart, you will see that all any Soul on your planet wants is love. What would happen if you truly experienced yourself in love's highest frequency? You would experience every player in their divine vibration of love. Your unconditional love would assist Souls to start losing their fear-based energy and move back into a conscious memory of their wholeness.

These Souls would then send the message, or energy, of love to other Cells/Souls of the collective that are going through the same experience. As love expands its color and healing sound vibrations, it breaks loose patterns in other Cells/Souls. In actuality, it is you healing yourself. This cycle would continually thread through the collective with the same patterns.

This would be similar to your Hundredth Monkey theory. Love's high-energy tone is capable of waking, or enlightening, other Cells instantly. They can awaken quickly because within they already have all of the components of a healthy Cell. Soon, you have a great, conscious vibration harmonizing together, a symphony.

It feels like you go through a difficult process when you incarnate to the Earth. This is because when you are in Spirit you are vibrating in a very high frequency of love, of completeness. When you incarnate to Earth you feel lost because it feels as if those on the Earth are speaking a different language. It seems different because the vibration or sound feels so dense, and there is no place to plug your light into, to mirror your own sound vibration back to you.

The collective emotional sound feels much greater than your own higher vibrational rate because you are in linear time, in form. Many times it is difficult for you to live in this emotional sound battlefield. This experience would be like vibrating in a beautiful healing symphony, and then all of a sudden you feel immersed into rap music. You feel short-circuited until you start healing and waking up and draw to you other Souls who are vibrating in your Souls' higher sound frequency.

When this happens, you are in harmony again. You once again feel home because you have like consciousness that is of your vibration.

As you align collectively with one another, a great healing takes place. The collective vibration of this higher sound frequency lifts you out of the old, karmic emotions. You then feel like you are back home with your real family, your spiritual family. This higher love sound threads through all dimensions of yourself and into the One heart of love.

Love's frequency and sound is much higher than any fear frequency. Love is beyond duality or separation. Love is!

Just think, if all of you light workers, or Souls, started vibrating in your highest love frequency, how quickly your world would heal.

Thought is energy, and you can create anything in your life when you understand the power of thought. When you truly understand this, you will change your world by changing your thoughts.

This is great power, and this is how your planet will heal and come out of duality. You are each other, and as you see others in their innocence and perfection, you will mirror unconditional love back to all of Creation. Love is and cannot be duplicated by false light. Love is an energy source, which has a power frequency and song so powerful that it can never be destroyed.

It is the highest power of all existence, or consciousness. Love is.

I ask that you watch your thoughts. If you have a negative thought, quickly change it to a positive. As you practice this, you are giving your subconscious a new job. It will enthusiastically assist you. As your mind starts to create a negative thought, your subconscious will automatically assist you to change it to a positive.

You will experience the great power that your thoughts have over your life and health. You will feel yourself much more joyful and happy. Happy, positive thoughts create a happy, positive Co-Creative life. Call on me and together we will Co-Create a world that vibrates in bliss and harmony!

"As you are blending back together, you are moving into a symphony, a musical of all colors blending into the rainbow of Creation. You are coming home together as One Cell and One Soul. This is Oneness."

Message from Archangel Raphael

CHAPTER 12

Archangel Raphael Speaks

I come to you now. This is Raphael. My gift to you is the healing presence of God/Creator. My assignment is to assist you to awaken into the healing frequency of your own God Source love.

I am assisting you through the ascension assignment by awakening the ray of green into your body's mind and emotions. All is color and sound. The sound for my green ray is the sound of the wind gently whistling through to the center, or core, of your Soul. My sound will clean and clear out old, stuck, karmic agreements and belief systems for you individually and collectively.

Call on me, and you will feel the heart of God/Goddess love fill your body, mind and spirit with ease, peace, harmony and humbleness.

I AM here to bring you out of separation from the original split from Source. When you first agreed to separate from the One Cell of Creation and take on many different roles throughout all Creations, you expanded yourself to awaken emotionally for the collective.

You were created in light and love, where you basked together in all colors and sounds. You were a rainbow symphony living in the breath, the womb and the ebb and flow of Creation. As the separation began, you started awakening into your own thoughts, feelings and emotions.

This was somewhat difficult because you had not thought

individually. All of your emotions were in the ebb and flow of God's love. You started feeling a freedom, and at the same time, fear in what you were feeling. You were not used to all of the emotions that were coming up.

For some of you the experience was very empowering, and for others, you felt like you had been pushed out of the nest too soon.

With this separation you felt great fear, and when you experienced your brothers and sisters feeling empowered as they expanded themselves multi-dimensionally, you started feeling less than, started feeling left behind like you weren't good enough, like something was wrong with you, that you were less than others.

Because you were also expanding yourself multi-dimensionally, you brought your hurtful emotions into all of the dimensions with you.

Although you were in an individual experience, your core, or beginning, was the One Soul, or Cell, of Creation. This Soul was your foundation, your umbilical cord to your Mother/ Father's womb.

The further you expanded yourself the less you could feel, or remember, your core roots. You started feeling abandoned by God, like you had done something wrong, like you were not in God's favor and felt like the black sheep, like God cared more for others than for you.

What actually happened was you were created in a rainbow color/sound musical of love. The colors were your breath, the ebb and flow of your foundation and beginning.

When the split, or separation, began, you were in the ebb of different colors. Some of you split in the red ray; others the orange ray; others the green ray, the blue ray, the yellow ray; all the colors of the rainbow and your chakra systems.

When you separated on the wings of the rays, you created what is now known as your Earthly chakra system.

Those who separated in the red or orange ray experienced different emotions than those who split in the green, yellow or white ray, which is the ray of the constant connection to Source.

This was not an accident. This was by agreement. Each ray has sounds and tones, and you had the choice as to which color frequency you would ride the waves of your Souls awakening.

And yet, in the frequencies of each ray's color are emotional feelings and experiences. As you split through the different rays, your Soul groups were created.

Each Soul has its own tone, or sound. Each color has many different shades and variations.

Now on the Earth your Soul groups are calling each other home inside of yourself. The many different variations of the colors are emitting a tone, and you are finding each other. Through the Ascension, your Soul group is continuing to expand itself multi-dimensionally as you are drawing to yourself the aspects of your tone that you had left behind in your descension.

You are becoming whole inside of yourself as you are ascending through all dimensions back into the One Cell/Soul and ebb and flow of Creation. You are awakening into the core and the ebb and flow of love, of God that is your beginning, your Creation.

As you are blending back together, you are moving into a symphony, a musical of all colors blending into the rainbow of Creation. You are coming home together as One Cell and Soul. This is Oneness.

Many of you are experiencing beautiful colors blending together, colors that are bright, beautiful and radiant. These colors are crystalline and are sending frequencies of sound into you individually and collectively. These are higher dimensional colors. You will continue to experience an activation of these amazing colors as you continue to ascend into higher dimensions of yourself collectively.

The crystal colors are activating coding in your Cells and are awakening your crystal DNA systems. This shift of consciousness is why you are experiencing so many people awakening spiritually. They are blending together again as rainbow systems and becoming One with the I AM mind and heart of God, of Creation.

In the original split, the Souls that agreed to ride the waves of the higher chakra, color, sound frequencies actually were holding the light, the silver cord for those of you that agreed to venture through the lower chakra system. The lower chakras carry the frequencies of fear and all emotions that the fear frequency creates.

For those of you incarnating through lower chakra frequencies, you must remember that you are also great Masters who have agreed to go into duality to assist many to understand emotional feelings that could not be experienced in the higher dimensions, or chakras.

You became the great Warriors, Shamans, and Wayshowers that have led the collective through duality and have opened "the light at the end of the tunnel" for all to move through.

You are all absolutely equal. Not one of you is better or more favored by God. You all took on your agreed upon roles and are coming back together sharing your great gifts and wisdom.

All of the havoc and darkness on your planet is the shift and awakening of lower frequencies from the original split of the expansion. As you are ascending collectively, your beautiful symphony of love, your light, is activating all the old fear frequencies that need to be brought to the surface to heal.

I suggest that you do not connect to the fear in your world. It is an illusion that is awakening and breaking up. If your collective light was not so high and bright, the fear frequency would not be activated.

Just as the higher chakra Beings held the light for many of you who separated through the lower chakra rays, it is very important that you continue to awaken and remember that you are the I AM source of love. Your agreement is to now hold this love and light for those who are still struggling to awaken.

As you are awakening beyond your Earthly consciousness, your beautiful colors and music have shifted you beyond your Earthly chakra system. This system is your core foundation while inhabiting your Earthly body, and at the same time you have shifted and awakened into the Creator's chakra system that vibrates through all dimensions.

There are many variations of this chakra system being downloaded to you now. The variations come from the different Soul groups that are awakening through other color/sound frequencies. All is well; connect to the higher chakra system that you resonate with because all of these systems connect the One chakra system, the One Cell/Soul of Creation.

The Creator has opened and awakened for all of you, the chakra in the thymus. The color of this chakra is turquoise. The thymus chakra is your roadmap to freedom. The aqua, turquoise color now runs through all of your systems and clears out the old, karmic map.

This is why so many people are now being drawn to and wearing this color. The thymus is your high heart and threads you through every Soul on your planet's higher self and consciousness.

I ask when you think of others, whomever they may be, to send your high heart turquoise color into their thymus. This is the chakra that the Creator's love and light continues to flow through and unites you together as One Soul/Cell.

As I mentioned, my assignment is to hold the green ray of healing for all of you.

My Ascension agreement through my green color/sound is to clear and heal old, karmic hurts and emotions for you individually and collectively. I AM to clear old prejudices and fears to break loose the karmic pattern between nationalities, religions, cultures and prejudices.

My green God Source ray dissolves the old hurts and prejudices that have created mental, emotional, psychological and physical sickness and dis-ease.

I am always with you. My green ray showers you and your world with healing energy. Call on me, and ask for my healing God Source ray of love to heal and dissolve all old fear-based sickness and dis-ease. You will feel me with you. Ask and you shall receive.

Thank you for allowing me to speak with you. I love you. I AM you.

Archangel Raphael

CHAPTER 13

THE CREATOR SPEAKS
THE LIGHT AT THE END OF THE TUNNEL

"This Earth is not dying as many are projecting; what is dying is the old, karmic structure."

Why are so many in other dimensions interested in the Earth? It is because the Earth is a hologram of death and re-birth. This Earth is not dying as many are projecting. What is dying is the old, karmic structure. As you look into a hologram, you see many different pictures depending on how you are looking into it. As you turn it a little you perceive each picture differently. This is now the Earth's consciousness, or story.

When you re-incarnated to the Earth, you came down in Soul groups. Each Soul group has its individual color and sound. The color-sound frequency is the consciousness of the group. The collective intention is to bring all Soul group frequencies together and create a rainbow color-sound symphony. As each Soul group's colors and sounds expand, they eventually will merge into each other, creating another combustion of light, like the big bang. This combustion will break loose frequencies from Soul groups, which are still struggling in the Shadow/Ego fear energy.

There is no past, present, or future. As you experience, know, and understand this, an activation of light within your Cells will stimulate the old fear programming. As this activation takes place, the light in your Cells will penetrate the old programming, pushing it to the surface. The fear programs then become easy to release and dissipate. As they are released, your Soul's color-sound, light song, crystallized structure is then re-activated into a higher frequency of light.

The Earth being a hologram is a screen that has had many movies, or plays, projected on to it. The many civilizations on your planet did not die; they are not lost. They did not become extinct. They played themselves out to the end of their existence, or death, of their learning experience. The Earth's slate was wiped clean again for the re-birth of the next play, or movie, to be projected on to it, to be able to play itself out to the end of its karmic agreements.

"The Earth is a time portal. It is the only planet where all reality or consciousness exists together simultaneously, through all dimensions."

Now, on the Earth, the outcome of these movies is going to be different. You, the light Ones have been in many of these plays and have played every character. Sometimes you were the victim and other times the villain, sometimes the main character of the play and other times an extra. You have played out every experience, feeling, and emotion possible. You are now in the greatest show, or play, to ever exist on the planet Earth. You have agreed to become One with the Christ AM consciousness, to activate your golden ray to assist the whole, collective consciousness, including the Earth, through the death, re-birth, resurrection and Ascension of all Creation back into the I AM of Oneness.

The light in your DNA is continuing to be activated, and your Cells are awakening into the Cells of all Masters who have gone before you. You are now expanding into your own light forms, which are vibrating in other dimensions. Many of you are in the awakening stages of remembering that you are the Masters who have gone before and that you opened the door for you - yourself, just as you are now opening the door for many. You are all moving into your One Cell structure of Creation. As you come together as One, your divine Matrix of light pulls the collective through dimensions and opens doorways for all to expand into higher vibrations. This is how the Ascension process works. Your Cells are re-connecting to the light Cells of yourself in higher dimensions. It's your own light that continually pulls you into higher frequencies of consciousness. It is your Cell/Soul remembering and creating a combustion of light, which creates a birth contraction. Every time you are in a contraction, you are in a collective emotion. As the light moves through and the emotional frequency releases, you move through a portal, or doorway, and into a higher color-sound vibration collectively.

Because the coding is in your DNA, there is no way that you cannot move through these portals into Enlightenment and Ascension. In the future, it is already done. As I said, you are going through a karmic death collectively, not necessarily a physical death unless your agreement for living on the Earth is up.

You are moving out of the duality time frequency paradigm. It is the pendulum swinging back and forth. Your agreement is to bring this pendulum back to the center, to the heart, where the mind and heart sing the same song: one of love, support, and freedom. You are at a pivotal point of this great balance and awakening. You have many Beings such as yourself who are from Creations beyond the Earth's understanding of time, who are on your planet now.

You and your planet are coming into a new season. Right now you are in a winter cycle when the Earth looks like it is dying. In reality, it is sleeping. Doesn't it seem like the consciousness has gone to sleep and that there is a shadow hovering over the light? Do not fear. You are in a rejuvenation cycle collectively and will see many more seasonal cycles of re-birth.

You and the Earth are hitting continual plateaus releasing collective frozen fear patterns. Because you have all of the cycles of all the seasons' elements within you, when your light activates the collective fear patterns, a combustible release takes place, which affects your weather. This is one of the greatest reasons that the weather and your seasons on Earth seem so out of balance.

Your emotions create an imbalance of the elements within you. Your collective, imbalanced elements then connect to the elements on the Earth, which create havoc, destruction, death, and re-birth. You could say the Earth is going through the hormonal imbalance of adolescence. As you, the Souls of the Earth, continue to balance your collective emotions, you will experience the Earth's elements coming back into balance, only in a higher vibration.

You are re-building to collectively emerge into springtime, where all is beautiful, strong, new, and fresh. You are moving into a springtime re-birth portal back into Oneness and Enlightenment. In winter, it looks like a death has occurred and yet all is inward, reflecting and taking time to re-connect and rejuvenate within its own cycle to emerge again. As you look at your seasonal cycles on Earth, this is the cycle of Creation. Old Cells' consciousness dies, and new ones are rejuvenated. You and your planet are aligned with the divine consciousness of Creation. Your planet takes twelve months to go through its seasons.

The Earth is the stage, or playground, where you, the inhabitants, can evolve. Because Earth is a Holographic Portal, the growth of consciousness of love and light can awaken and expand more quickly here than on any other planet. You are Beings who are on the brink of total awakening. As this awakening occurs, you will bring many Souls through the birth canal with you.

You are absolutely not going to lose your great Mother Earth. Every time your world comes together in like consciousness and sets the intention collectively for a better world, this new intention sends a wave of light into your Cells, moving you into, through and beyond negative, fear karma. This re-threads you into the future of light.

"You are now coming together through the heart's love energy to Co-Create a better world for all humankind."

My intention now is to assist you out of duality by you experiencing and understanding the shadow, so that as a nation and world you can come back with each other as one world under God with liberty and justice for all. The ego shadow needed to be exposed and brought to a head, which has been done. You, as a people, needed to understand that the shadow is its own entity and has a great purpose in assisting the awakening and healing of this planet.

As the coding in your DNA has been activated beyond time, you will find yourself as a collective becoming more conscious.

Light bubbles of Knowingness are constantly being turned on inside you. You, as a collective, are coming together in your highest purpose and intention for the best of all people.

In the next few years you will continue to see many of the old structures breaking down. You are coming into a new lifetime without physically leaving the body. You need a new foundation for this lifetime. The new foundation is your Mother Sophia and I, the Creator. We are your spiritual parents of a higher consciousness and are the guiding heart-mind for you and your planet. As your DNA coding is being activated and you continue to awaken spiritually and merge back together as One light and One Spirit, you will remember and know you are the Cells/Souls of a larger consciousness. In human form you will still have your personalities, and yet the lens through which you see others and the world will be much different. You will view all through a lighter lens: one of love and compassion.

You will want for others what you want for yourself.

You are coming back to one another, opening your hearts and Souls to assist each other to have dignity, self-respect, and to become whole again. You will see your brothers and sisters as you and have compassion and the desire for the highest for all.

From your awareness of the larger picture of consciousness, you can shatter the ego shadow. You are now coming together through the heart energy to create a better world for all humankind.

Through the shattering of your perceived security and belief systems, you are now uniting collectively. It may seem this union is one of fear, but it is one of merging your light together through intentions, to take your power back from all fear agreements. Now as a collective conscious Being of people, you are in the first steps of accessing your emotion of repressed anger and injustice.

This anger is not to destroy; it is to release old, collective belief systems and others' control over your lives. It is to release injustice and powerlessness and to awaken your own God source energy of love and to merge together to Co-Create a better world for all.

This new consciousness is starting to be demonstrated in many countries. You are now agreeing to take your power back, to move out of the victim role and into the re-structuring and re-building of a New World, of the true Garden of Eden. Look how many of you have become conscious of how precious the resources of your planet are. You are collectively coming together to preserve these resources for future generations.

"You and Mother Earth are co-habiting in the greatest role ever played out on your planet. I smile to Myself when you are being told you are lesser Beings; you would not have so much intelligence interfering with yours if you were not very important."

You have a great purpose. That purpose is to love yourself! When you can feel and know your own love and magnificence, your divine piece of this Ascension Consciousness will come to you, meaning your gifts - your spiritual tools and purpose - will awaken within you. What you are searching for is searching for you also, but many times it cannot find you because you are trying to live someone else's purpose, or someone else's perception of who you think you are supposed to be.

As you love yourself, you love all that is. As you love all that is you start spreading love, light, health, peace and freedom to all Souls. As this Soul/Cell healing takes place, the birth of this new higher vibrational Creation becomes easier. It is the difference between a natural childbirth and one that requires the use of forceps. Either way, this birth is taking place, because you have already gone through the birth canal of the Ascension agreement. It is being activated in your DNA. As you understand the process of natural childbirth, you will know that you can breathe into the cycle and experience the love and magnificence of the child being birthed by you. This child is the birth of the collective consciousness beyond duality. You are assisting each other through the birth canal of Enlightenment, Ascension and Oneness.

After this job is done, many of you will continue to stay on the Earth to hold the light memory for those on the planet. Others of you will leave, not out of fear or tiredness, but because your job is done, and you can go back home into the heart of love, of Creation, before it is time for your next assignment. Through intention ask your heart to become One with My heart and feel yourself fill with the love, light and the beautiful music of your Soul's Creation.

CHAPTER 14

QUAN YIN

I am with you now. This is Quan Yin. I come to you as your sister of love, compassion, mercy and grace.

Just as all of you on the Earth have your own divine purpose so do we in spirit.

We all have our purpose and chosen mission to assist the Earth and all of you Earthlings to blend together into one race of love.

Many of you are aspects of us that have lowered your vibration, frequency, and incarnated to the Earth to become the portals of light for us to be able to download our frequencies through. Many times we do this by the agreement of your allowing us to verbally speak through you. In this agreement you are actually channeling higher aspects of yourself, which are us.

Other times you agree to open your heart and to become the portals that our frequencies vibrate through.

We may not speak, or channel, through you verbally, but you are the embodiment of our Soul's agreement, our Soul's color, sound and musical frequencies that you and the inhabitants of your Earth need to create a whole symphony of love.

Each one of us has our chosen field, or frequency, to assist you through the Ascension doorway.

You are our portals of light that we are vibrating through. You, the portals of our light's intention send the energy to all that you come in contact with and also ground our energy into Gaia, your beautiful Mother Earth.

Each one of us Masters and Archangels have color frequencies that match our Soul's mission.

Each color has a sound, or tone. As we become One consciousness, which we are in the higher dimensions, we create a symphony of sound of love so beautiful that it actually breaks all sound barriers of fear, and all you can feel is love, peace, harmony, compassion, forgiveness and grace.

Many times as you are shifting dimensions within yourself, you will actually hear different sounds and tones and as the tones' frequencies blend together multi-dimensionally, you will move into complete silence, peace and grace.

As you are shifting multi-dimensionally within yourself, you may hear the birds singing more beautifully and experience all of the magical colors of water much brighter and feel the fields of energy that nature so beautifully shares with you. You may experience the expanded energy of sunsets, sunrises and rainbows and feel the colors are beyond any earthly color you have ever experienced before. Everything is brighter and more colorful. You will feel the light frequencies of the colors penetrate your bodies and systems and awaken the feelings of love, grace and aliveness that you have not remembered. The colors are awakening the frequencies of sound; your Soul's song and your bodies are singing and resonating with the beautiful music of Creation. This music of love is healing your Souls and awakening your bodies and systems into the rhythm of love. Listen and breathe in the beauty that you were created in. This is your homecoming.

All of us have our own assignments of which energy frequencies we are holding for your planet's evolution. All starts with love. Love heals all and from love of self, you move into all other frequencies that are the embodiment of love.

My gift to you and your world is love, compassion, mercy and grace.

I hold the light/love frequency of the feminine to assist you to have compassion for yourself and all beings on your planet. Love and compassion move you into a state of grace.

Grace breeds peace, and you experience all around you and in your world in its perfection and from this comes peace. Peace within creates peace throughout. You become a live generator of love, compassion, peace and grace. You experience your world through the lens of love. You experience all existence through the lens of all Masters and Angels that are assisting you and your world into one blended race of love. You become the collective consciousness of all our beautiful colors, music and intentions for your world.

You move into the safety of your inner child where your inner child vibrates in the heart of love. Your heart becomes our heart, and our higher selves merge together as we blossom into the OverSoul's heart of your planet.

Just as you have a higher self, you have an OverSoul that carries the knowledge and higher wisdom of every lifetime, time lines and experiences that you have ever gone through. Your journey has not only been on the Earth. Your Soul's journey has taken you through many star systems, planets, galaxies, universes and Creations.

Your OverSoul carries all of the gifts and knowledge that your Soul has awakened into from the beginning of your Soul's journey. Your OverSoul also carries the wisdom of your future selves.

Remember in the higher dimension, there is no past, present or future: no time. You exist throughout all consciousness because you are all consciousness.

All information, understanding, wisdom, and knowledge is available to you through your OverSoul. Your higher self is your guiding light, your connection to your OverSoul.

Just as you have an OverSoul, the Earth has an OverSoul. All consciousness has an OverSoul. This is also what you could call higher dimensional wisdom. Every dimension merges into higher dimensional frequencies. There is no end to dimensional awakening because there is no end to Creation. When you understand or move into, click into, a dimensional frequency and your system downloads the wisdom, or consciousness, of the dimension, you then move into a higher dimension within yourself.

As you are ascending through dimensions, codings in your DNA are continuing to be activated. You may not understand what is being activated, but as your bodies and emotions continue to shift, higher memories of you are awakened and you open to a knowing within yourself. You see and experience the world's Soul's awakening through a higher lens of perception.

Your world also has an OverSoul. We, the Masters and Angels of your world's Soul's awakening and Ascension, blend our Souls/Cells together and bring our vast knowledge and merge with your Earth's higher self.

As we merge together with the Earth's higher self, we become one with the OverSoul of your planet.

We, the Masters and Angels, are on assignment to assist your Earth through the Ascension portal, home into One love.

We have done this many times with other planets that were ascending into enlightenment. We have the tools to move Gaia and all of you through the birth canal into freedom. We are constantly monitoring the contractions of the birth that you and Gaia are collectively going through.

We see that you are going through the birth canal beautifully. But, if we see it is not possible to birth this beautiful starship home safely, we will certainly perform a cesarean birth, meaning, the cesarean birth would be the cutting of all karmic cords and contracts (contractions) for the Earth and you, the Cells and collective consciousness, and lift her into safety.

You are not going to lose your planet. We won't allow it. Gaia is a special child of the universe. Her purpose is very great. She is a hologram planet that has allowed all karmic civilizations and cultures to play out whatever emotional patterns, programs, hurts and imbalances that needed to be understood and released.

Now on Earth, you have every karmic agreement that has ever been awakened reliving emotional experiences, breaking contracts, and releasing old, toxic emotions to move you through the tunnel of light into freedom together.

This is the greatest role Mother Earth has ever allowed to play out on her planet.

She is such a gift to us. We will not allow anything that is not safe to happen to her. When you truly understand Gaia's journey and all that she has gone through to assist all of you into freedom, you will have great honor, love and respect for her. You will truly see her as a massive living Soul that is mothering you all out of duality and through the birth canal into One love, into freedom for all.

Absolutely everything is energy. Your world and all of you are constantly emitting energy frequencies.

Imagine giving birth to a child. Through which frequency would you want this child to come into your world? Of course it would be love and safety.

Mother Earth, Gaia, is birthing all of you. It is very important to assist her through the birth canal with thoughts and intentions of love, peace, harmony, forgiveness, compassion and grace.

She is giving you the greatest gifts that your Soul has ever received. She is birthing you home into the nucleus of love, of Creation.

She is your starship, and you are the engine, the propellers, and the wings of this beautiful Earthship.

Watch your thoughts, feelings and emotions. Be conscious of what energy you are aligning with, what morphogenetic fields you are matching and merging with, and what energy you are putting out to the world.

You are Masters and Co-Creators. What do you want to Co-Create for yourself, for your biological families, for your Soul families and for your world?

You have a choice as to what energies you desire to ride the waves of Ascension through and what frequencies you choose to support Mother Earth with.

Love, forgiveness and compassion are your freeway home.

The energies of fear, conflict, anger, blame, and victim will breed more fear and bring clouds of darkness around you.

When vibrating in fear, the energy you are putting out to the world is one of worthlessness, not being important or valuable enough to receive and vibrate in the safety of love.

Behind every emotion of fear, blame, anger, hatred, and injustice is a hurt child within you that does not feel worthy of love. From this worthlessness, you will bring people, places, and circumstances into your life that will mirror your fearful, self-righteous behavior. Their energy patterns will spark your energy, and you will receive from them more invalidation and worthlessness.

When your intention is love, healing, forgiveness, compassion and Oneness, the frequencies of the intention will download through all of your frozen emotional energies and start dissolving old hurts and injustices from all of your bodies. As they dissolve, you will begin to feel love for yourself and others. Love is who you are. Love is your birthright – your Creation.

All within you and around you that does not vibrate in love is old, karmic energy that has re-surfaced with the intention to dissolve the fear and re-awaken and remember your own Creation of love.

You are not alone on this Soul's awakening journey. We, the Masters, Angels and Wayshowers, are always with you. Call on us! We are waiting to extend our hands and hearts of love to you.

We cannot do this coming home journey without you. We are you! You cannot do this journey without us. You are us! We are all on the same team. Our gifts are that we are not living out karma; we vibrate beyond these awakening lessons and are shining our light for you to remember.

As challenging as your journey may seem to be, there are still Souls leaving us to incarnate to your Earth now.

There is great excitement to be able to clear out karma in one lifetime and to awaken on the Earth into the higher spiritual Beings that you already are in the higher realms of spirit. What a gift to be a magnificent spirit, a spiritual guide in a physical body.

And of course you have incredible Beings of light that have already cleared out karmically and are coming through into your world as amazing children. They are being born fully conscious; they already know who they are. They have not forgotten the higher wisdom and knowledge that they intend to share and awaken your world into.

You also have many star children being born onto your planet who are carrying the frequencies and light languages from the many planets and Creations that have already ascended into enlightenment.

All of these incredible children are the future of your world. Listen to them! Have eye contact with them. Allow their wisdom and higher consciousness to penetrate and awaken you through your eyes, the windows of your Soul.

Vibrate with their love, joy, innocent wisdom, and the higher intelligence that they are bringing to your world.

See that your world is in good hands, in the hand of love, the hands and heart of One Creation of Love. Focus your intention on your new world of love, peace harmony, joy and freedom for all and it shall be.

Love, forgiveness, compassion and grace are my gifts to you. The Dalai Lama is a great companion of mine. He is the light of love, forgiveness and compassion for your world. He is a beautiful portal of love, light, joy and innocence and emits these healing energies to your world. You are great companions to many beings of light from many dimensions that are assisting your world. Align with them. Become the portals, beacons of light that are shifting your world into Oneness.

I love you. I am you. We are One.

Quan Yin

CHAPTER 15

GAIA

I come to you now as Gaia, the higher self of Mother Earth. I am speaking to you, and Mother Earth will also speak to you.

I have many stories: the history of the Mother's journey as a great vehicle beacon of light. Mother Earth has so proudly assisted many civilizations to play out their agreed upon lessons - the lessons that their collective consciousness needed to learn to move themselves out of duality. This does not mean that they moved out of duality. It means that their agreement was to go into duality to experience fully how their ego selves can create fear, conflict, confusion, separation and death.

Mother Earth is now allowing the greatest stories ever to play out on Earth. Many of these stories are actually polluting and violating her bodies, such as the dis-ease that many of you on the Earth are experiencing in your bodies and systems.

Just as you as a human species have great vibrational imbalance in your bodies and systems so does our beautiful Mother.

Mother Earth's Soul was brought from the Planet Maldek after the ego became so great that it actually blocked the feminine spirit's existence. Because the Earth's Soul is feminine, her light no longer had a like frequency to vibrate with, to mirror back to her, her feminine energy of love, life force and compassion. The intentions of the civilization's agreement was to learn to balance the male and female, the heart and ego, so the light and shadow could move out of separation and competition and could merge together in balance as allies, to support each other in the highest good for all.

The opposite happened. The separation between the male and female became so great that the male ego of fear, greed, and control actually temporarily put the feminine light out and the body of Maldek died.

An evacuation took place, and the Souls that were aligned with the Soul of the planet's healing were lifted off and taken back to their planet of origin.

The night before the evacuation, the Soul of the planet, that is, the Soul of Mother Earth, was actually lifted and brought to this planet that you now inhabit.

When her Soul was brought to Earth, it was very much guarded and protected until she could integrate into the grid systems and fully embody the planet.

Since that time the Earth's Soul has allowed many civilizations to play out their karmic learning agreements, and the higher Angels, Masters, Brotherhoods, Sisterhoods and even the Creator itself has constantly monitored the growth and awakening consciousness of the different civilizations that have come to Earth.

The hierarchies of light are protecting Mother Earth and will not allow another disaster to happen on Earth.

Mother Earth herself is also monitoring the frequency and consciousness that is awakening. You can see her releasing blocked energies and not allowing people to become too comfortable or complacent in their roles. She is waking people up individually and collectively by removing many comforts, like homes and seeming securities. She is not allowing her physical or energetic bodies to become so dense that she cannot breathe.

From her eruptions, people are waking up to the importance of life, love and family. All else is temporary and can be taken at any minute, but love is eternal.

When the Soul's awakening experience of Maldek happened and Mother Earth's Soul was brought here, she lost her body, but her Soul did not die. She re-incarnated to the Earth as her next assignment to assist you in your Soul's awakening.

Just as her Soul did not die, Souls do not die; your Soul has never died. She left her body; her body did not survive the experience, but her Soul is very much alive, stronger and so much more conscious and powerful. She will never allow herself or her body to be taken for granted or violated on that level again.

Can you see that your Soul's cycle is the same? You never die. You leave a lifetime and move home into spirit to understand and integrate the experiences that your Soul agreed to learn from the lifetime that you left behind.

Your Soul has learned from every role and experience that you have ever incarnated into.

Now on Earth is the greatest role you have ever played. Mother Earth's Soul's agreement is to be the strength for all to ascend through all dimensions beyond karmic learning experiences and back home into the heart of love – home into the ONE Master Cell from which all were created.

She is a great Master Mothership that is the strength and body to move you through all Ascension portals and into the awakening of your own inner Master.

As you vibrate together as Masters, you will Co-Create Heaven on Earth: a Heaven on Earth that will love and support all genders, religions and species where all will live together in equality, peace and grace. Call on me! Align your higher self and intentions for Mother Earth's healing with my higher self. Together we will be the wings of love that will glide our beautiful Mother through all Ascension portals back home into ONE heart of love.

CHAPTER 16

Mother Earth

This is Mother Earth. I am honored to be the Mother, the Master vehicle that you have chosen to incarnate on. I am also honored to ascend together with you through all time lines and dimensions back into the heart of our Creation.

Yes, I speak of our One Creation. Just as you are Cells of a larger body, Soul/Cell, I, also with other planets, am the Cells of a larger body of consciousness, or Creation.

As we are ascending many of you are re-connecting on the Earth with so many incredible aspects of yourself that are playing themselves out in other people's bodies. Your light is shining so brightly, and your Soul's frequencies, or songs, are activating each other. You are feeling a kindred spirit relationship with each other. You feel like you have always known each other. You are coming home.

As we are ascending, we are moving through many veils, or time lines, within ourselves and are shedding the old skin (patterns, hurts, belief systems): anger, fear, injustice and many older, frozen emotional stories. We used to vibrate with each other in the old emotions. Our energies, or etheric bodies' systems, were like electrical magnets. We would vibrate in the frequency of the pattern and instantly draw the same pattern or opposite side of the pattern back to us.

This was our agreement: to vibrate with each other in karmic patterns to activate the patterns collectively. As we are moving through the unconscious mind, the subconscious is assisting by holding us in the pattern until it becomes so tiring and unbearable that we want change.

I speak to you of us because yes, I am also aligned with other planets as we are assisting each other out of our karmic, emotional patterns. We are also Souls. Our Souls reside in the center of our bodies and our hearts just as humans and other species do.

Every planet has feelings and emotions. Our Souls communicate and support each other through our chosen journeys, just as you do. All is consciousness and connectedness.

You, the Cells/Souls, that live on our planets communicate with and assist each other. We, the Souls of the planet, also communicate and assist each other. Galaxies communicate with each other; they are a body of consciousness. Universes communicate and activate each other. We, all of Creation, are always expanding ourselves and assisting each other to grow into the memory that all is one. Absolutely nothing is separate. We all exist together through what you could term, or call, past, present and future.

For those of you who shed your veils through past life clearing and Soul retrieval, the lifetimes that you call past are as real as this one. The energies, or patterns, have threaded into this lifetime creating another similar story only with different players. The pattern is still there, and you bring people, or players, and experiences, even sickness and dis-ease, to you as the gift to clear the old emotions.

All is now! Because you are One consciousness, as you clear the history for yourself, you start unraveling the history's emotional hold for all. Imagine the collective emotion held as a big ball of string. As you shift and clear the pattern for yourself, the ball of string starts unraveling for the collective.

Whatever you see or feel within yourself, you can also witness the emotions shifting and unraveling for the collective.

Nothing is separate. All is one. As your vibrational frequencies expand and become higher and lighter, you emit a sound frequency and align collectively with others of the same wave length. Your collective musical symphony then sends the frequency into me, Mother Earth, and clears my lay lines of my own Soul's karmic history. As the ley lines of my/our planet clear, our love fills my heart and feeds my Soul. I then send out, or emit, frequencies of love and harmony.

Because my Soul vibrates with other planets' Souls, our beautiful love symphony activates the Cells/Souls of other planets and shifts them into a higher vibration. If other planets are already enlightened, or carry many of the tones that I am emitting, we align with each other in that frequency and sing together as One higher Soul, or planet.

We/you are always evolving. Nothing ever stays still or is the same. When you truly understand and become conscious that you are me, that you are the Cells of me, that we are each other, you will look at me through a different lens of consciousness. You will know how magnificent you are and how your thoughts, feelings and emotions affect the history chain of evolution, you will be very conscious as to what you choose to put out into the world. You are the world; we are each other.

We are all ascending together and remembering that we are one. It is not just me, Mother Earth, and you, the Cells of me, which are ascending. All consciousness is evolving together. How could it not be when we are not separate from each other? We are each other.

The Ascension shifts us through all dimensions within ourselves. As we clear and shift into higher dimensions within, we actually lift all consciousness into higher dimensional frequencies. Along the way, we meet within ourselves many loving aspects that have been trapped, or were vibrating, in collective fear or unconsciousness. We also meet our own shadow. Sometimes we meet our shadow through a "Dark Night of the Soul." As we move through the darkness into the light at the end of the tunnel, our shadow that was aligned with the collective shadow disengages itself and becomes our light's ally.

Again, this is a collective journey. All is shifting. As we meet many aspects of ourselves that have awakened, we merge and shift with our higher selves, our inner children and our inner partners.

Our inner partner is the aspect of our self that has been waiting for us to awaken enough to merge with us in love and wholeness.

If we are male and yes, some planets have a male Soul, we will bring our inner feminine aspect to us. This balances our male and female within. Our feminine can then merge with our male, which assists us to open to higher aspects of spirit.

If we are feminine, we will bring our healthy inner male aspect that will hold us and keep us safe as we merge with each other into one balanced frequency of love.

From this balanced frequency of our male and female vibrating in love and support, we will draw to ourselves balanced relationships from the outer.

For many, if your intention is to have a partner other than your inner partner, you will draw a magnificent Being, a physical partner who will love and support you. This will be another homecoming.

Just as you have partners, we, the Souls of planets, have partners.

As we moved through the 2012 doorway of Ascension, I merged back together with my beloved. He is not a physical planet, but an etheric planet where many Souls that leave Earth go for more of an understanding and completion of their Soul's journey. We, spirit and I, call this planet "my beloved Father Earth." He has been holding the light for me, Mother Earth, since my beginning on this planet.

He is etheric, and his mission is also to assist us in our Ascension and evolution. He and I are now back together and are the ebb and flow of each other. His energy balances me and mine him. I feel very loved and supported as our male and female energies propel us, this magical starship, through all dimensions of ourselves and back into One heart of love, of Creation.

Remember, we are One, and you are a magnificent Being of light. You are the Cells of a larger body of consciousness, and your light and wisdom turns the light on for other Souls/Cells to remember their magnificence, to become healthy, whole and to vibrate in love, peace, harmony and grace for all.

Call on me. I will send my love to you as we continue on this incredible journey of our collective Soul's awakening. We are coming home.

Mother Earth
Mother, Father Earth

*The chapter from "The Creator Speaks" explaining Mother Earth's reunion with her companion Father Earth is in the back of this book: "Mother & Father Earth's 2012 Reunion."

"What an incredible Master you are to have chosen this lifetime to shift and clear karmic frequencies of fear throughout all of Creation and back into balance of the male and female throughout all history of your Soul's journey."

Message from Archangel Gabriel

CHAPTER 17

Archangel Gabriel Speaks

We are One consciousness. All that you see in the world is you. Yes, all that you see is mirroring you in some way. Even those that you fear are you. We are One consciousness that has split out of form and are playing ourselves out in many different ways and forms.

Some of you took on the role as great light Wayshowers.

Others took on the role as playing extras – not in their personal life. In your personal life, you are always the main character, producer and editor. But in the larger Earth play, you may be holding frequencies for others that have taken on more dramatic roles - both the light, dark, shadow and in between.

This is a lifetime of completion, of coming full circle, of moving out of karma individually and collectively.

The only way to break karma's hold of duality is to break and clear your own duality, grief and separation.

This starts with forgiving and loving yourself. It is difficult to love yourself when you still have self-doubts and judgements. As you forgive yourself, you will find a level of self-acceptance and self-love that you could not even imagine exists within. As you forgive and love yourself, you will only see and feel love and forgiveness in the world regardless of what side or character anyone is playing.

Every thing, event, and story you experience around you is a reflection of your own inner turmoil and light. Your own inner light has activated frozen emotions within yourself that need to be dissolved and healed and loved.

As you free yourself from past karmic energies, discretions and agreements, your lens of perception for yourself and the world will change dramatically. You will move out of self judgement, fear, control and greed.

This healing shifts you into the larger picture of life and Creation. You will want for others what you want for yourself, regardless of what role or side they are on.

Your lens of perception will be one of compassion and forgiveness for all Beings; human and other.

Your self-love and forgiveness actually melts the glue (frozen, fear emotions) that collectively holds the world in fear.

As you clear the old energy, you transmute fear to love for yourself and the collective because you are the collective Oneness of all of Creation.

You move into higher vibrations of yourself multi-dimensionally and align with Masters, Teachers, Wayshowers and Angels of light that vibrate in all of the beautiful colors of Creation. With them you assist the world and all consciousness to shift beyond duality, out of separation and back into love, light, peace and harmony throughout all of Creation.

You become the light and remember that you are the ones that you have been waiting for and move into the Ascension portals and wings of love that will glide your planet and all Beings home into the heart of love, of Creation.

What an incredible Master you are to have chosen this lifetime to shift and clear karmic frequencies of fear throughout all of Creation and back into the balance of the male and female throughout all history of your Soul's journey.

I love you and thank you for allowing me to assist you to glide home on the wings of love and into the greatest role your Soul has ever played: the role of complete freedom for all.

Archangel Gabriel
(Wayshower)

CHAPTER 18

St. Germain / I AM-Violet Flame

I am St. Germain. I come to you as the eternal flame of life, of your existence. I carry the flame for you and all of Creation.

My flame is violet, and as you call upon and become the flame of the I AM, of all knowing, you will be vibrating in the heart of God's love. My I AM presence is the core of your Soul's flame. This flame will clear and cleanse away all energies that are not of the Creator's highest intention for you on your Soul's journey.

As you are shifting through all time lines into the core of your Being, you will experience that the I AM flame is the thread of our ONE existence. The flame is of eternal life and is the heart and core of Creation.

The I AM thread is the one heart of God's love. As you call upon me, my flame will instantly align you with the highest purpose of Creation, of your Soul.

When you chant the words I AM, you will feel all of your Cells awaken into the presence of pure love.

The tone of the I AM is in your DNA waiting to be activated. Every tone has a color. As the I AM frequency is activated, the violet flame will cleanse away old, karmic patterns, hurts and injustices.

Allow the I AM to be your mantra. When your mind is busy with old thoughts and memories that no longer serve you, chant I AM. Replace the old with your higher vibrational frequency, and you will feel a cleansing, a clearing, and an uplifting of your thoughts and emotions.

Your mind will become the mind of God. You will lift yourself beyond your earthly agreements and vibrate in the higher knowing, or purpose, of your Earth's journey.

The I AM violet flame stimulates your crown, pituitary and pineal glands and opens and aligns your brain with the brain, mind and heart of God. When you call on the I AM, you align yourself with the beauty and harmony of the One presence in all universes.

The I AM "One presence" is waiting for you to Co-Create for yourself a life of love, compassion and freedom.

The I AM will align with whatever your intentions are and will assist you to move into the morphogenetic fields of your frequencies.

The I AM moves you beyond time where all is energy and blends together in One consciousness.

When you call on the I AM you immediately become one with the I AM violet frequency. The violet flame will wash away the old misconceptions of yourself and of God, of Source.

The I AM is pure Source energy. It is very important how you use this energy. Whatever you claim as your truth, the I AM presence will assist you to download and awaken within you.

If you claim to be I AM the Source of love, light, peace, harmony, hope and grace, you will merge into the collective field (morphogenetic field) of your I AM intention. The Cells in your body will hear the sound, or tone, of your intention and will awaken and align themselves with the Cells within you that carry the same vibration.

Because we are One consciousness of I AM that threads through all of Creation, your awakened Cells will align with other people's Cells that carry the same intention.

Your body's Cells become one with the Cells in other people's bodies and create a collective frequency of the intention.

Everything is energy, and the I AM energy is the highest that you can call upon and awaken within yourself. Whatever you state, call upon or intend is already floating around the ethers somewhere.

Your Cells will vibrate in the collective energy of the thought that you put out to the universe.

This is called the morphogenetic field. Morphogenetic fields are Cells vibrating together in like color and sound frequencies. Your body's Cells actually support whatever your thoughts and intentions are. As they move into the morphogenetic fields, they support other people's Cells that vibrate in likeness. We are One consciousness and energy field.

The consciousness and field carries many different colors and sound. Whatever thoughts you put out will align with the color and tone frequency of your thoughts.

I suggest that you use the I AM presence wisely. As a Master, Co-Creator, your thoughts create an energy field that aligns with similar fields, and you constantly bring back to you like vibration.

Chanting I AM will align you with the higher heart of love, the collective love in which you were first created. You will align with the Source of all that is. Your Cells will rejoice in your Soul's song as they come home together in love and safety. They will remember that they are love, that they are the heart of love, that they were created in love. The I AM love presence will turn on the memories of your Soul's birth, the beginning of your existence, of your Creation in the heart of Mother/Father God/Creator.

As you are reading this transcript, continue to chant I AM. How does your body feel? You can chant and read at the same time. Your mind is always busy. What you will feel as you chant I AM is your body will respond and your mind will quiet down.

The I AM will lift you into the truth of who you are, which is love and peace. You may even feel yourself move into the silence of love.

I speak to you of the power of the I AM, which is total presence of the highest consciousness of Creation. In the center of this consciousness is silence, is the omnipresence of Oneness, of Creation.

When you understand the power of the I AM presence, you will choose very wisely what you align yourself with.

Whatever you align your I AM thoughts with will manifest in your outer world.

If you claim "I am tired," "I am bored," "I am sick," "I am old," "I am unlovable," "I am fat," "I am ugly," "I am stupid," etc., your Cells will align with the energy of your thoughts, and you will re-affirm to the universe that this is your truth. You will move into the morphogenetic fields of your I AM intention and will be supported only by other people with like thoughts, or consciousness. You are each other. You are One. Thoughts are energy, and your Cells respond to thoughts and turn on your painful emotions that resonate with your thoughts. Your DNA Cells already carry old memories of these hurtful emotions.

Your unhealed emotions will activate the frozen fear emotions within you, and your Cells will awaken and vibrate in the color/ sound frequency of your thoughts and belief systems. You will then align with other people who are putting out the same frequency, and your body will break down in sickness and dis-ease.

Think very clearly when using the words I AM. What are you aligning yourself with? What color/sound frequencies are you riding the waves of Ascension on?

This is the lifetime that you have agreed to come full circle. Every experience that you have gone through in this lifetime has an emotional attachment, or frame of reference, in what you call past. Because of this you have every feeling and emotion that your Soul has ever experienced within you.

These emotions are constantly being activated, and you then vibrate in the morphogenetic fields of the emotions.

This is constantly happening even when you are not aware of it.

You are an amazing musical instrument that is always playing itself with the collective consciousness of your world.

When you understand this, you can choose which frequencies you desire to align with, what color/sound frequencies you want to vibrate in. You will always bring like frequency back to you because your Cells will be vibrating in the morphogenetic fields of your I AM emotions.

My assignment in the Earth's Ascension is for my violet I AM flame to cleanse your world karmically. As we come together as one I AM presence, our divine love will transmute and clear karmic fear frequencies out of any form, or story, and back into the isness of peace and harmony.

Together, we can do this. This is our agreed upon mission. Consciously connect your I AM flame together with mine. Collectively we will assist to bring this beautiful starship planet Mother Earth and all of her inhabitants through the Ascension portal back home into the heart and arms of eternal love and freedom.

Call on me. Become one with me. I AM always with you. I AM you. We are One. I love you.

St. Germain

CHAPTER 19

THE CREATOR SPEAKS
RE-BUILDING A NEW WORLD –
RIDING THE WAVES OF FREEDOM

"You will experience a great love and appreciation for the simpler things in life."

I say to you, "You will re-build!" This re-building will come from a very conscious place of intention, of humbleness. At this time, you are still in a place of anger and injustice and are now taking your power back. The only way you can do this is for all to be exposed so that you can understand what is going on in America and your world. That has been done. You will no longer be victims being led around by false powers. It may seem like everything is continuing to fall apart; but actually, you are emerging in a higher consciousness as you continue to move through your collective emotions.

You will experience a great love and appreciation for the simpler things in life. You will not be so wasteful. You will no longer be a disposable society.

You will be more appreciative of the Planet Earth and for what everyone has gone through together. You will have more meaning in your life. You will return to the importance of family and relationships.

As all of you are being brought to your knees together, you

are seeing each other again and reaching out to one another. You are rowing your boat together, this boat being your new intention for your world. You will get through. You are returning to the true Garden of Eden where you will be standing naked with each other. This nakedness is the absence of your patterns, programs and old perceptions.

The old structure, or paradigm, must come down to be able to build a new one; that is happening now. With the economy strong, you did not know who you were. You thought you were your homes, cars, boats, TVs, etc. From the collapse you have the opportunity to experience yourselves again, to slow down and feel your hearts. You are now opening up again in prayer, many times on your knees in desperation.

I hear you; I am holding your hand as you continue to walk through your darkest fears. Together we will persevere and move through this false reign of shadow power, of greed, of too much emphasis on materialism.

You are now filling your Soul with Spirit, with Creation. On bended knee you are gathering the strength to go on. You are coming together and carrying each other over the finish line back to the heart, back to what is important, to what is real, and that is love. Love is the only truth and safety that there is.

You have heard the song 'Without love you have nothing at all.' This is true. When you are on your deathbed and ready to leave your body, the only thing that will be important to you is love. If you have not had love, you will feel a loss that is unimaginable. You will not be thinking about your homes, cars or materialism.

Your whole life will go before you, and this will be your judgment day. It is not Me who will be judging you; it will be you judging yourself. What did my life mean? It went so quickly. Did I make a difference in anyone's life? Did anyone love me? Did I love others? You will be in a higher vibration and viewing your life through the lens of My heart and your pain.

You are now collectively in the karmic death, and your life is moving before you. You are now asking yourself these questions. I hear you crying, crying out for love. Where is love in my life? Where is my divine partner? What is my Soul's purpose? I feel like I can't live on the Earth any longer without love or joy or happiness. I feel like I can't live another year like this. I say to you I am with you, and as you continue to open your heart to the heart of Me, you will have love.

You are love; you were created in great love. As you continue to surrender the illusion of love (which is really fear of love), all karmic veils that hold you back from love will dissipate, and in front of you will stand a brilliant mirror of your own love and magnificence. Everywhere you look or turn, you will have and experience love.

If you are longing for your divine partner, he or she will be standing there to take your hand. Your Soul's higher purpose will magically appear to you. You will feel so at One with Sophia's and My love that Our hearts together will open your consciousness to all possibilities of love. Through self-love you will be able to receive the love that you have waited for, that you already are.

It is then that you will be grateful for what you and your world are going through now. You will feel blessed that you had the opportunity to move through the collective "Dark Night of the Soul." You will feel weary and somewhat beat up but in a good way. Your lens of perception will be much higher, and you will feel a freedom within yourself that you did not know to be possible.

You will be more integrated with your higher self and with Mother/Father/Creator. You will know and remember that you are Spirit in a human body and that you have come to the Earth to experience freedom. From this Knowingness, you will feel great joy and happiness and will actually be able to laugh at yourself for all that you thought was so important.

You will feel happy to be alive at this time of transition; you will feel grateful for your process because your life will have more meaning. You will be grateful to be back in the new Garden of Eden with all of the great Masters in Spirit as well as those on the Earth.

You will have merged through dimensions as One consciousness of love in many different bodies, with many different personalities, in many different color-sound frequencies that have merged together in a beautiful symphony of all Creation. In the new Garden of Eden, you will want to share with one another all of your great gifts. Your consciousness will be higher as will be your lens of perception. You will see through the eyes and heart of love. You will experience your cup full instead of half empty.

In the future, this is already done. Your job is to continue to unravel what isn't and you will morph into what is. You signed up to be on the Earth at this time. It was your Soul's agreement. You knew all of the losses that you would be going through individually and collectively. You signed up to be on the Earth to experience the greatest time of transition ever and to collectively move out of karma through all inner doorways into the 13-13 Christ awakening within yourself and eventually into freedom.

You have the opportunity to release all karma and to live your life through intention, to Co-Create a new life, a New World consciousness and a New Earth.*

I want you to breathe in your beautiful future into the now. Feel My words and love for you. Allow your body to take in your new story, your new script, the one that you signed up for, and that you wrote before you came down to the Earth.

Set your intention for this to be, and it shall. Connect your heart and intention with My heart and intention.

Together, We will ride the waves of freedom through all doorways into the 13-13 within yourselves and into Enlightenment and Ascension. You are the ones that you have been waiting for.

Thank you, and so it is.

---

*The 13-13 are the Christ Ascension numbers. If you chant 13-13, codings of the Christ consciousness, which are in the DNA will activate and awaken.

CHAPTER 20

THE CREATOR SPEAKS
CO-CREATING HEAVEN ON EARTH

"Now is the time to Co-Create with Me the love and joy of life, which is your birthright."

You have had many incarnations on the Earth plane, where you came to an end of what your Soul could comprehend, or understand, at the time.

There was no failure and never has been. You played out end times of the opposition between the heart and Ego. When that was done, in whatever form it took, the civilization came to an end, and you moved back home to understand the whole play. All of your incarnations have been plays so that you and the collective could act out and release any illusions, or misunderstandings, from the original split from Source.

When the play came to an end and you moved back into Spirit, you were able to look at the lifetime that you were coming out of as if you were watching a movie. It was then that you could experience yourself clearly. Because you received many impressions from your Earth parents, surroundings, and environments, you were then able to see clearly how these influences orchestrated your life's decisions.

From the play becoming very clear, you chose to re-incarnate to the Earth again and re-write your new script, to complete the lessons that your Soul needed to learn or did not complete.

When you were able to see and experience all of the movies that you made from your agreed upon lifetimes, which kept you in fear-based realities, you became more conscious in re-writing the new script for your next lifetime.

As I speak to you now, it is to give you My word anew. My greatest desire is to bring you back home into the heart of love.

My heart, arms, mind, and higher consciousness is open to you to remember who you are so that you can return home, within yourself, within your heart, into self-love.

Every role that could possibly be played out, you have already played. You need not struggle to remember who you are. There is no need to play the villain or victim to understand duality. You are every experience. You have great wisdom and knowledge within yourself.

Now is the time of great awakening. Your job of duality is done. You have served this great awakening well. Collectively, all that needs to be known is known. This Knowingness now has to be brought forth into the light, into your own light.

Sophia, your Souls' Mother, and I are shining a light so brightly that your path home, through the heart, through love, will be much easier.

Much of the disturbance on your planet now is because the light's I AM frequencies are penetrating all of your fear illusions. This light is shattering the Shadow within you and the collective.

You are in a death and re-birth cycle at the same time.

You have a beautiful, brilliant mind. Use this mind in alignment with My mind and heart. We will Co-Create a civilization so brilliantly light that the light will dissipate all confusing illusion.

Now is the time to Co-Create with Me, the love and joy of life that is your birthright. My greatest desire is to mirror My love and light back to you so strongly that all on your planet will have spontaneous enlightenment. I want all of you to remember your own magnificence.

Your planet can quickly evolve out of separation if you set the intention for this to happen. Thought is energy, and when all set their intention, through the feeling of your heart's love, to have a better world, we will Co-Create Heaven on Earth in all life forms.

I am now sending light frequencies to your planet. You and the Mother Earth are through the birth canal of Ascension.

The light is coming down and opening portals of consciousness within you and throughout all Creations. These light downloads are continuous. The light cycle activates codings (portals of light) in your DNA that bring you into a higher consciousness of awakening, perceiving, and understanding within yourself.

Every time this birth contraction happens, you are moving through the womb of Creation and into a higher light of the I AM of All That Is.

When the light hits, you will feel many old feelings and emotions surface so that you can go through them and pull the roots up. Your feelings and emotions are from every incarnation, individually and collectively.

Through this great awakening, you might feel uncomfortable within yourselves. You will sometimes feel nauseous and have vertigo, and your bodies will feel out of balance. You will be losing your identity of who you thought you were, or what you thought you were supposed to be.

Goals that you had set for yourself may no longer seem real or important. You will have great confusion and feel like you are losing your memory. Your taste for food will change. You will not know what you want to eat. Nothing will taste good. As your vibration is being turned up, you must put higher vibrational foods and energies into your systems. Your bodies need food as energy or fuel. You must bring into your bodies the food that vibrates with you now.

All of your bodies are losing their old memories and need to know that all is well. Talk to your bodies as you would a child. Let them know that you love them and honor them. Thank them for being a beautiful home for you in this lifetime.

Acknowledge your beautiful bodies. They need to be loved and honored just as you, the adult, do. As you acknowledge your beautiful bodies, they will feel very peaceful, loved and grateful that they now have the opportunity to be free.

Your bodies carry all of the memories of your mind and need much love and support. Love them to health and into their optimum potential.

You may have days when you have great energy and then the next day none. You will feel like you are on a roller coaster ride.

Go with the ride. Go with the flow. Your bodies are detoxifying and re-adjusting to the new vibration, if you need to rest or sleep, set time aside to do this. Be in the moment of now. Act from now.

Who you were in the past is gone. Live in the now. Do not judge yourself for what you are feeling or going through. Love yourself. Accept yourself. Honor yourself, and be kind and gentle with yourself. Honor yourself for your willingness to come to planet Earth and for being a part of this great awakening. See your cup as full instead of empty.

No one has failed. You are on the Earth again with all of your fellow travelers to become totally awakened.

You agreed to come to the Earth with other great Souls

with a wiped slate, clean of all memories of Enlightenment, of Ascension.

You went into the depth of the Shadow collectively. You agreed to begin totally unconscious and very quickly moved through the karmic wheels collectively to re-awaken all consciousness into light of enlightenment, of Ascension.

Jeshua was the Being of My light who agreed to re-incarnate to your planet and open the door for the Christ that is you, to awaken. You are the Christed Ones. You are the Second Coming of Christ. The golden light on your planet is very bright. You are in the Golden Age, the Second Coming, and within your DNA systems codes are now being activated.

Every time light frequencies hit your planet, the light activates codings in your DNA individually and collectively of the Second Coming of the I AM of All That Is, and lifts you into a higher frequency of the Golden Ray of consciousness.

The Golden Ray is Ascension, Enlightenment, and peace on Earth. This is love, happiness, joy, freedom, and abundance on all levels. The Second Coming is the Christ I AM consciousness of light and love, awakening, and Co-Creating Heaven on Earth. This is living in the true Garden of Eden, in My Golden Temple, in the Heart of all knowing, of Oneness, of Grace.

Call on Me, the Creator, Jeshua and Magdalene. We are you. We are One Heart shifting into the memory of our ONE Soul of Creation.

CHAPTER 21

COMING HOME – THROUGH INTENTION

"Your intentions will continue to change and expand as your perceptions of consciousness becomes higher."

Now is the time to set your intentions. Thought is energy. You, the light rays, lead the way for many others to find their way through the darkness and back home into the light. Think as you, the collective rays of light, come together in Oneness, the light will be so bright that it will open the passageways for many Souls to move through the portals and awaken into their I AM selves.

As you come together in Soul Groups and set your intentions collectively, your heart's love, light, and Soul's songs will create beautiful harmony to soothe and heal your whole world.

Thought is energy! Co-Create a new paradigm. Hold this frequency for all to connect with and vibrate in. This new consciousness will penetrate the hearts and Cells of many other Souls.

They will feel hope. This hope will give them energy to move through the doorway, or birth canal, into the Golden Age of innocence.

After your Soul Group's intentions are set, put your collective intentions into Sophia's and My Golden Heart and expand them through all consciousness. Other Souls will feel the frequency and awaken into higher vibrations.

As you collectively move into a higher vibration of light and sound, the sound will break loose old, frozen, emotional patterns, or grid systems. When these old patterns start breaking loose, it is most important to hold an intention to create a new grid system, or paradigm, for the collective.

When an old, emotional pattern breaks, a new frequency must be downloaded in its place. Think, feel and hold your higher frequency's intention for your subconscious to accept the love and light frequency as its new truth.

Be firm in your intentions.

Your intentions will continue to change and expand as your perceptions align with a higher consciousness. Do not be confused by this. As your consciousness becomes higher, so do your perceptions, which create new intentions.

I love you. I honor you for your agreements to come to the Earth to bring yourselves into Self-Realization, Enlightenment and Ascension, collectively. Now is the time you have been waiting for since the beginning of the great illusion of separation. You have never been separate. You have been taking a nap. Now you are waking up together as the Christ I AM through all Creations. You are remembering who you are. You are magnificent Beings of My light, love and Creation. We are not separate; We have always been and will always be.

As you continue your journey home inside of your heart and Soul, you will feel yourself in the sunrise of all consciousness awakening. The unconscious will become conscious for you. You will vibrate in total Knowingness, which is Oneness beyond duality and fear illusion.

Open your hearts to My golden love. Continue to surrender into love, for love is All That Is. Allow love to permeate your whole Being. It is the power that will lift mountains and dissipate all fear-based frequencies.

Many of you are great Teachers and Masters that walked on your planet and prepared the foundation to open the door for your brother Jeshua. Now you have recycled back (re-incarnated) to the Earth again and are the Masters who are preparing and holding open Ascension doorways of the Golden Light, of the Christ awakening for others.

As many walked before and opened the consciousness for you, you are now walking before and awakening consciousness for others. You are the Wayshowers of the Golden Age of Ascension.

Walk humbly, My children. Know who you are. Walk with great love, peace, and grace in your heart. Know that all is you, and the more you love yourself, the more you can love and accept others. Know that I am always walking with you, and I am continuing to shower My great light upon you to guide you home.

Manifest yourself as a Co-Creator with Me. Do this by going into your Golden Heart Temple and expand yourself through all Creations of light. This light will assist you to feel a higher vibration of love. You will feel great peace and comfort. You will feel like a child wrapped in a golden blanket. Open your hearts and minds and talk to Me. Open the energy lines of communication with Me. I love you. You are My child, My children, My great, great, grand-children of love.

If you ask, you will receive. You may not feel My answer at first, but the more you communicate with Me, the more you will feel My frequency. As you do this, you will move into direct communication and Oneness with Me. I will speak to you. I will shower My love on you. I will show you your way home.

I am your guiding light. I love you ! I AM You! We Are One!

I AM. I AM. I AM.

CHAPTER 22

THE CREATOR SPEAKS-
MIRRORING YOUR SELF-LOVE TO
FREEDOM

"You are always the source of your own Creations."

You are always the source of your own Creations. If you are in fear energy, you will create many forms of reality to mirror that back to you. If you are in the victim role and angry with Life, others and Me, being the Creator Being that you are, you will bring many players in the collective consciousness to mirror the victim back to you. As this happens, you will constantly set this scenario over and over again until you are tired of playing the victim. You will then find ways to come out of that role and create another role, or play, for yourself. With each role, or play, that you are in, you will always find your chosen support team on the Earth, which will cheer you on in your role. When you are tired of the role and no longer get energy from it, or perhaps your support team, or audience, is leaving, you will find another role to play, once again bringing your like vibrational team to you because they are you in the same play.

As you cycle through all of your Souls' growth patterns, your classes become easier for you. You go through a graduation into another realm of consciousness. As you move into this higher understanding, you continue to bring to you like consciousness, other light Creator Beings who support your growth and graduation.

You will hold this new frequency of sound and color and draw the same vibration back to harmonize with you. As you harmonize with one another in a higher frequency, this new sound continues to break the barrier to old frozen fear lifetimes, or misalignments.

As you move through this frozen energy, you start connecting to higher aspects of yourself in all dimensions. As your light becomes stronger, it activates old hidden, or frozen, aspects of yourself that were left behind, or stuck, in other plays, or lifetimes, in other dimensions.

I know I am repeating myself, but I want you to know and believe that there is no such thing as failure, only a transformation of not knowing into Knowingness. You hear much spoken of the Knowingness. As you start moving beyond these lessons, you move into the Knowingness, beyond what you could call karma, or time frequencies.

You are moving out of the separation between the male and female, of the heart and Ego, of the light and Shadow and are merging back home into the One heart of Love, of Our One creation.

You are great Creator Beings, and have the opportunity to assist Me, Creation to tame the collective Ego through love. Love is the foundation for All That Is. As you continually love and appreciate the Ego and its role in your life, it loses its power and surrenders, or transforms, itself into the light consciousness of self-realization. I love you and thank you for continuing to cycle through your old karmic patterns and agreements, to assist the evolution of the collective consciousness home into freedom.

When you have had every experience one Soul could possibly have, you will not have judgment towards others. You will have great caring and compassion.

What you will experience inside yourself is peace. When you truly understand that you agreed to go through these lifetimes, the veils of illusion will be lifted. When you came into this lifetime and other incarnations, you came in with amnesia. You couldn't remember much of your Souls' other experiences. You needed to forget to remember. If you remembered, you would not understand the lesson emotionally. It is only through feelings that you truly understand an experience. Someone can tell you an experience, but if you have not gone through it yourself, you truly do not know.

You can, from your mind, try to intellectualize it through similar experiences, but you will not truly understand until it becomes your total reality. You agree to immerse yourself into an experience to be able to understand another Creator Being's perspective. There are only perceptions based on your life's experience. When you go through all experiences that a Soul can travel through, there are no more perceptions based on experiences; there is only love.

There is much talk on your planet about unconditional love. You cannot love unconditionally if you still have judgment, or blame, towards other Souls and circumstances. They are gifts, the teachers that have agreed to mirror to you, your old patterns that need to be healed, cleared and shifted. As you move beyond judgment, you move beyond time and see others' magnificence as yours. As you go through every experience a Soul could travel through and you release any emotional attachment, you move beyond blame, or confusion, and blend with all cellular structures in total love and Isness. Self-love is your birthright and freedom.

A Self Love technique:

Look into the mirror each morning and into your own eyes, the windows of your Soul. Tell yourself, "I love you. I love you. I love you. You are safe in love. We are now with our real parents, Mother/Father/God/Creator. We are safe with them."

Do this again before you go to bed at night. When you get in bed, go to sleep with these thoughts of self-love. Your subconscious will open the door to more memories of love, past, present and future. Because Like attracts like , you will bring more opportunities for love into your life. Remember, everything is a mirror of your own reflection. Love, love, love, and love yourself some more. Love is your purpose, your destiny, and your salvation! Whatever the question-Love is always the answer!!!

CHAPTER 23

THE CREATOR SPEAKS- SEASONS OF YOUR INNER AWAKENINGS

"Allow yourself to be in the flow, for you are emerging into a beautiful butterfly with My wings of freedom."

Your life and body are like the seasons. None are bad or right or wrong. Life is a continual cycle.

Death and rebirth are your Souls' cycle, as it is the body's. On your Souls' journey, you will continue through many experiences. Sometimes your season is one of spring, where much energy bursts forth with a new confidence, a new beginning. You experience this as birth. Springtime is a rebirth, or rejuvenation, of your consciousness. Summertime is a time of light, awareness and letting go. Autumn is a time of remembering, of gratitude, giving thanks and forgiveness, and of assimilating all of the year's experiences. Winter is a time of deep reflection; a season of introspection, to go within yourself to truly experience who you are and an opportunity for great change and setting intentions.

Winter

In the winter of your life, you are in a reflection cycle.

You have the opportunity for deep reflections, to experience who you are, what you want in your life and what is important to you.

As you let the light shine into your Souls' awakening, you will move further into your Souls' purpose.

The winter season of your life is very important. It is when the greatest changes can take place, if you allow it. As all of what you believe or perceive is stripped down or away, you actually have a stronger connection with the source energy in which you were first created.

As you sort out old beliefs of what you call past and set new intentions, great growth takes place. Winter is a time of setting the intention for a new foundation. All is still, and you can start to see more clearly.

As you allow yourself to go into the emotions, honor them, support them, give them a voice and allow them to tell their story; they will start unraveling and releasing. From this release, you will feel great freedom, peace, and a stronger sense of enthusiasm, and purpose. You will have the strength to go forward again.

As you go through this release, your frequency becomes higher.

Every time you release who you are not, you have more room within to experience the magnificence of who you are, to expand your light into self-love and to awaken into the beautiful color-sound vibrations of your multidimensional Soul.

Springtime

Springtime is a time of new beginnings of joy, happiness, light, and freedom. If you look at nature, you will see that after wintertime, the trees have stronger roots, flowers are blooming, and there is so much life force bursting forth. Birds are singing again. A great awakening, or a birth, of a new consciousness is taking place. Because you have all of nature's elements within you, and your bodies are aligned with the seasons, you will also feel the joy, happiness, new hope, and birth of this season.

Springtime is a time of rebuilding, of action.

Your vibration is higher and you get to rebirth all of your new ideas and perceptions. As you vibrate in your higher knowing and understanding, the birth of your new ideas burst forth from within you, the Master and Co-Creator of your intentions.

Summertime

Summertime is a time of light and awareness. You have given birth to your new ideas and consciousness. You are vibrating in your Souls' higher, sound-color frequency. From this higher place, you will continue to draw back to you like consciousness. The sun is shining, and within you, your great inner light connects to the vibration of the sun's vibration.

Many times you decide that what you enjoyed in the past is no longer for you, or you feel that people you enjoyed before, you no longer have anything in common with. These people are not wrong, as you are not wrong. You have grown, and your vibration is different. You no longer have the same vibration or sound-color frequency exchange with these people. Many times, it means you have completed what you agreed to go through with these Beings karmically. As you move out of these relationships, you make room for new relationships and new experiences in your life. In actuality, they are not new. Nothing is new for you in this lifetime. All whom you meet and experience, you have been with and have experienced before. You are here to complete with one another in love.

Summertime is when the light within you has been activated so that you can see and experience all very clearly, not from old fear emotion but from the emotion of love, self-respect, and forgiveness.

Autumn

In autumn, it is most important to slow yourself down and reflect on all of the miracles of your life, the first being the miracle of birth, and to thank yourself for your willingness to, once again, take on a body and come to Earth to sort out all experiences through your own time cycle. It is a time to look at the growth that you, your Soul, has been willing to go through, to bring yourself back to the awakened, or enlightened aspects of yourself multidimensionaly.

Thank yourself for being strong enough to journey through what you call time to assist the collective consciousness back into one love-light vibration. Thank all who are in your life for their strength and dedication to assist you to see and love yourself wholly; thank them for mirroring back to you all aspects of yourself that you need to love and accept. Thank yourself for all the great healing, awakening, and self-awareness, which you are now experiencing and for all aspects of yourself and of your personality that are already in full manifestation or bloom of love.

Autumn is a time to love all, to thank all, to look at the year and see all of your perceptions of struggle, and to love them: to love all that is you.

When you continually see all lessons as gifts and thank them, you start shifting them from fear into Love and gratefulness. As you download Loves vibration into the patterns and emotions, they start breaking up. This will free you into a grateful frequency.

As you become aware and start giving thanks for the story you have been playing out for so long, the story starts dissipating. It no longer has any power. It unthreads itself from the collective story and frees you to remember who you are, which is a magnificent aspect of our One creation playing itself out to the fullest expression, beyond duality, or fear. "Thank You" is a very powerful expression and energy source. It has a vibration that breaks the fear control frequency. This vibration connects to the highest consciousness of Creation. The vibration of "Thank You" goes back to My heart awakening with My Beloved Sophia. As My feminine heart opened, all I could feel was gratefulness. From this gratefulness, came My true experience of loving all of you, the Souls of My Creations. I was able to experience the love of Myself totally and from that place, I was able to love you totally because I created you as One with Me.

Start giving thanks even when you don't feel or believe that you have anything to be thankful for. Again, you will break the stuck energy, and soon you will start feeling grateful, your heart will start feeling more love and you will truly feel thankful. The simple words "Thank You" plug into other Souls' love-light patterns and songs. They no longer feel judged, or ashamed, or feel that they need to protect themselves by being right. They feel seen, acknowledged, and validated by you. As you give thanks for everyone and everything, your energy starts breaking loose from the patterns, and you can then move into the feeling, or true experience, of forgiveness.

You are in a rebirth cycle of a collective love beyond your conscious memory, or understanding, at this time. Allow yourself to be in the flow, for you are emerging into a beautiful butterfly with My wings of freedom. You are the seasons of Creation – you are Me, all of Creation.

Your "inner" Internet system is truly a consciousness of the divine mind, or a higher mind and heart of Our One creation. You are the seasons of all Creation. Relax now; know that you already are All That Is.

Give thanks for every season of your life, and you will find yourself opening many doors to the higher love and light of your Being. Remember, your seasonal emotions vibrate with the seasons of your planet. As you allow yourself to flow through the seasons within yourself, your higher vibration will start balancing out the erratic weather patterns that you are now experiencing on the Earth. **And so it is!**

CHAPTER 24

I AM

"I AM every thread and vibration of existence. I AM the vibration of every cell in your body. I AM all Creation. How you decide to use Me is up to you."

I AM. I AM. I AM. I am the trees, the birds, the springtime of your life and consciousness.

I AM death and re-birth. I AM the wintertime of your life. I come at unexpected times, and I take the jewels from your life to assist you into a higher understanding, or unveiling, of yourself. I AM All That Is; all that is constant, death and re-birth, winding down and re-building, awakening.

Your whole lifetime now and all lifetimes have been a continuous cycle of death and re-birth. Death is a closure to one experience, and re-birth is the next step past the closure.

There is truly no death, only constant re-birth. As you come to an end of a chosen experience, you either learn the lesson or not, but you always come to a closure of the chosen agreement.

Sometimes, the closure means you must leave the body to go on the next adventure of your Soul's journey. Some Souls cycle very quickly. Others take more time to grow, understand, and complete before moving to the next required experience. All experiences that all Souls have agreed to go through are to understand, release, and to free themselves from karmic emotions, to move back into the core of My Beingness, of the I AM of All That Is!

I AM All That Is and all that is not. I AM every breath you take and every breath you do not take. I AM every thread and vibration of existence. I AM the vibration of every Cell in your body. I AM all Creation. How you decide to use Me is up to you. You can use Me in all of My light power and existence, or you can use Me to feed and empower your pain, your Shadow.

I AM your laughter and joy. I AM your fear, sorrows, and regrets. I AM All That Is. Nothing exists without Me. I AM the core of your existence. I AM your Mother-Father God Creation. I AM the frequency, the mind and the heart of God awakened into you. I AM the bloom of all knowing, as I AM the total bloom of you.

I AM the sun and the moon. I AM all elements. I AM the Earth and the stars. I AM all cultures and all religions. I AM new beginnings and old endings. I AM the wind. I AM the ocean. I AM the water, and I AM the air that you breathe. Without Me, you cannot exist. I AM all Creation.

You see and experience All That Is through your perceptions of Me. Your perceptions of Me come from your direct experience of all collective emotions. You could not hold on to your old perceptions if you did not have others to align, agree, or mirror back to you your beliefs.

You are in a holographic consciousness. As I exist throughout all consciousness, you exist through all consciousness. You could not see yourself, or know yourself, without Me, for you are Me. I AM the life force in all existence. You could not know yourself if you did not have the Shadow aspect of My I AM, to mirror back to you, your reflection of light.

You could not know your Shadow without your light. You could not know your light without your Shadow. All lifetimes of your Souls Awakening needed polarization to awaken and balance all consciousness of the collective I AM.

The I AM frequency of your planet is now in the highest light-sound vibration that has ever been. This frequency is turned up beyond the original template of the Shadow-sound frequency.

This is what is happening on your planet now. The old template that held the groove of your existence on your planet is worn out. Your I AM consciousness has been stuck in the old sound-music template. You and I, the collective I AM, have turned the vibration up high enough to move the needle of the I AM beyond the template frequencies.

This agreed-upon happening is moving you beyond old time zones, lifetimes and dimensions where you have believed or experienced yourself vibrating in separateness. My I AM frequency is moving you, all light and Shadow aspects of yourself, beyond time.

You are now co-existing and vibrating in all dimensions simultaneously. You are now vibrating with yourself in parallel realities, universes and lifetimes. All I AM is coming together, and your light-sound I AM frequencies are breaking loose all old beliefs, fears and perceptions.

If you could see My I AM in all consciousness, both light and Shadow and all beautiful color-sound frequencies in between, you would be able to experience yourself in all of your glory, for all is you. I AM the glue that holds you together. I AM the emptiness in your heart waiting to once again be filled up with love.

When you see all as My Creation, you see all of who you are. You are powerful Beings of My I AM. I am assisting you to awaken: to vibrate in your highest I AM Knowingness. In this I AM comes total magnificence. You remember and know all in total love, compassion and acceptance, for all is you.

I know you, for I AM you. I love you, for I AM you. I see you, for I AM you. I AM. I AM. I AM. I AM the I AM of All That Is!

APPENDIX I

"We are each other's love, flow, inspiration and strength.
We are inseparable; we are One Twin Flame Soul's Song."

JESHUA AND MAGDALENE'S LOVE STORY

The Second Coming of the Magdalene – Christ

I am with you now. This is Jeshua. Our journey has been long and hard, – quite intense. Wouldn't you say? We are all coming home together. We are one. All that I am, you are, and more. I went before and opened the passageway for you to follow.

When I say you are more, it is because you are the collective Second Coming of the Christ consciousness. When I walked before to open the door for you, I was also walking in the collective, but you, the Souls of Creation, did not yet have a high enough vibration to remember you were Me in the highest.

There was great fear and speculation of My Being. This is because the magnitude of My light and love mirrored your light and started creating an awakening of love, of hope. When this happened, the old fear-based Ego structure became afraid of losing their power over you. We have now come full circle; you and I have come home together, and when We walked together through the 12-12 doorway, you moved beyond the karmic coding of oppression and into the freedom of your Soul's awakening.

It is then that you started opening to all choices of free will to Co-Create your new lifetime and to re-write your script. I strongly suggest that you now start consciously writing and intending your script. Because there is no past, present, or future, as you re-write your script for your new lifetime on Earth, you are sending the intention into what you call future and bringing it back into your now. As Our Father explained to you, you are now emerging into a new lifetime without physically leaving the body. You are emerging into the butterfly of freedom. You are moving out of your cocoon of old programmings, of old beliefs, and are merging together as one beyond time, beyond story and into the Isness of all that is. The doorways to Heaven have been opened for you, from within yourself, from your heart.

Set your intention now for your new lifetime on Earth. Set the intentions for yourself, for one another, for the collective, and for the Earth. Ask and you shall receive. Intention is prayer; know that you are all that is, and it is your birthright to claim your wealth of abundance for all, on all levels. Give thanks that it is done, and it shall be.

I wish to speak to you of My divine feminine, My heart, My Magdalene. She has always been and still is the light of My Being. She held the love and light for me as I moved beyond karma for the collective. Her feminine love held the door for My heart to continue to open and expand beyond any time frame and back together with Mother/Father of Creation.

Just as Sophia opened Our Father's heart, Magdalene held the love for My heart to continue to open, so that I could connect to your hearts in Oneness and expand Us into all of Creation, into enlightenment and Ascension. On the Earth Plane, this seems like a long time coming. And yet, in Spirit, it is but a blink of the eye in Our journey together. Many of you have been with Me on other planets or Creations, as We brought the consciousness beyond time into Enlightenment, Ascension – Oneness.

Our agreement now is to bring this Holographic Planet Earth

into direct alignment with the Central Sun's grid system. As We do this, each lens that you look through will be one of peace and appreciation for all that is. Just as our Father could not move into total alignment without Sophia opening His heart, I could not have fulfilled my plans, or contracts, without Magdalene, the heart of Me, and you cannot do it without your collective heart awakening to guide you home within yourself. Now is the time for this awakening. It cannot not happen, for the coding is in your DNA. You are being activated to awaken into the color-sound of your Souls' Song individually and collectively.

Magdalene and I also have come full circle, and she is now emerging into her Soul's higher purpose and mission - not just to hold her love and light for My heart to open and stay strong, but to hold the love and light for all of you, to now feel safe in your feminine. In the past, it was not time on the Earth plane for her to be in her full bloom purpose, and now it is. Along with Mother Mary and other feminine priestesses and goddesses, she will continue to guide the collective heart in the safety of love through all Ascension doorways into the balanced Feminine/Male Second Coming of the Christ Consciousness.

Just as she held the love and strength for me on my path, I am holding the intention of love, light, and strength for her to now guide you. Magdalene and I are already in total balance of one another. We are each other and flow in and out of each other's heart and in and out of yours like the ocean waves breaking, then building up again, each time creating a stronger union of balance between the female and male within you, individually and collectively.

Contrary to some perceptions of Magdalene's and My union, We had agreed to go through all of these great cycles of awakening together. Magdalene was not a victim, just as you are not a victim. When I was on the Earth, it was not appropriate for us to share our great love for each other openly with you. The consciousness was not such that the feminine was safe to be in a leading role position, and now Our heart is awakening into the feminine.

Just as you are playing out all karmic imbalances for the male and female collectively, Magdalene and I did the same. She knew she would not be able to be acknowledged as the love of My life until this time in the Earth's history. It was all planned by agreement. She knew she was incarnating into a difficult role for the feminine and that when the appropriate time came she would emerge again to assist in the great awakening of the feminine heart. Although she is not in physical body, she is more with you now than when she was on the Earth.

Your consciousness is now high enough to receive her. Mother Mary went before as the symbol of the virgin and opened the door for Magdalene to now go before you, to give you permission to open your hearts and bodies and Being to the sacredness of the feminine sensuality and sexuality, for the sacredness of intimacy between a man and a woman. She is also opening the door for the sacredness of love and intimacy between all Beings. Whether this love is between two women or two men does not matter. You are now moving beyond the identity of all forms, which as humans you were programmed to believe was love. You are coming back together in love. You have played all roles, all identities, and now you are all coming back together in love beyond gender, religions, and beliefs. This is by a collective agreement, or contract.

Magdalene and I knew before We physically met that We were being prepared for each other. She actually studied with my

Mother Mary in Egypt in the Temple of Isis. After Magdalene and Mary's reunion, our Mother Sophia and Father Creator assisted them both through many priestess initiations, to prepare Magdalene's vibration to be able to complement mine. She had a great role as my divine complement, to hold the sacred feminine energy for Me to be able to move the collective of Us through an awakening pattern of enlightenment and Ascension. Through the many initiations, my Mother, Mary, was able to hold the vibration for My beloved Magdalene to be able to hold the vibration for Me so that I could hold it for all of you.

After their initial meeting and through the initiations, Magdalene and I were in constant contact with each other spiritually in higher dimensions. When We met at the well our union was already so strong that as We came together in person, there was an explosion of light between Us that fused Us together as one Being of love.

Because We had been connecting spiritually, when We met in physical form, there was an instant marriage of Our energies coming together in love and the intention of Our higher purpose. After the explosion of energies between Us at the well, Magdalene had a difficult time holding her balance. I took her hand to hold her up and to assist with her balance. The following day, Mother Mary performed a marriage ceremony in physical form for Us that was brought forth from our Father Creator. It was that same night that We lay together for the first time in physical form as man and wife. We were sealed together as each other's Beloved.

She was the light of My love, My strength, and My will through the rest of My days on Earth, as she still is today. We are each other's love, flow, inspiration, and strength. We are inseparable; We are one Twin Flame Soul's Song. Just as

Magdalene and I came together as one, many of you now have been communicating with your divine twin flames in spirit and are drawing yourselves back to one another in physical form on the Earth Plane.

Mary Magdalene was not a prostitute as the church had portrayed her. She was and still is a very high priestess and prophet. She is now assisting in healing the rift between the Feminine and the Male. She is teaching and assisting many in Isis, Magdalene initiations, and is bringing much wisdom to the Earth from ancient mystery schools. Just as Mother Mary has made many appearances around your world, and has healed many from her presence, Mary Magdalene is now channeling love, light and wisdom through many and is appearing and healing many through our Christ-Union of Love.

My Death, Resurrection and Afterlife

There are many versions of My end times on the Earth and I say to you, all are correct. This is because you are living in a hologram of many end times of karmic completions. Depending on what Soul group's contract you are experiencing life through is the end time version that you will most resonate with and believe to be true. You may have one end time perception as your truth, and as you continue to grow in consciousness you may expand beyond that perception's color-sound vibration, move into another wheel of the matrix and merge together with another Soul group's Song. You have the opportunity to eventually blend together in all Soul group's Songs and into all matrices of Creation. From this place, you will have moved beyond any story and into the presence and a Knowingness of Magdalene's and My union of love, strength, and Oneness of the Second Coming of the Christ consciousness.

You will be in the Song of Isness where the story will not be important, only the love. This is the place beyond karma where you experience all endings as truth, and yet as illusions, for whatever is needed for each Soul group's completion of their story. You will feel great honor and love for all who have agreed to come to the Earth, to move through whatever lens of perception their Souls needed to learn from. You will be able to be with any religion, spiritual group, or belief and feel the Oneness with them all.

After my crucifixion I went through a karmic death for the collective. I did not die for your sins as has been said, in fact, I did not physically die. I died karmically for all of you to be able to move into a higher vibration together. Through My resurrection and re-birth, I opened the doorway for you to start questioning your own mortality. I intended for much confusion to take place. Confusion creates uncertainty. Uncertainty allows you to start asking questions; for you to think, to ponder about the larger picture of Creation. As I ascended, the light was so bright that it mirrored the higher self and Over Soul of Magdalene and My intention for the Earth. This intention has taken many Earthly years to manifest itself into a collective form for the Feminine to awaken the heart of the Male consciousness.

Many of you light Masters are very aware of this awakened consciousness. Now that it has awakened into form, you are collectively moving out of form and into a higher experience and expression of love into Isness.

You could say that I lived for you. I lived for you to remember your own love, light, and magnificence, and to remember that you are God, that you are Me. Through karmic, collective intention, you have created the consciousness of your Earth today and as you are now remembering yourself as God, as the Co-Creator of your own Creation, you can recreate all consciousness to vibrate in Heaven on Earth.

As I said, I did not physically die. When I arose from the tomb, my light body, higher self and Over Soul opened the door for the collective to move through the illusional veils of separateness. Later when all were looking at the magnificent light show of My Ascension, the human aspect of Me walked into the crowds, and I watched my Ascension with you. I then turned and walked into the next step of my Soul's journey on the Earth.

After My death, resurrection, and re-birth, I was seen in many places on the Earth, and it is believed that I lived on in many different places. This is true, for I am a Master Soul and can split my energies to be in many places at once.

Just as God is all over your world and vibrates through you and through all religions and beliefs, I am that also. How can I be seen throughout many places in your world at the same time? How can I heal many people in so many different places? It is because I am the Over Soul of your Planet as is My Magdalene, Mother Mary, Lucifer and his beloved partner, Ascendra. Yes, Lucifer is an aspect of my Over Soul. He is the carrier of the Master Shadow that creates duality. We are all aspects of the same Master Over Soul. This is why Mother Mary can be seen and witnessed through many different religions or lenses. She is able to heal many all over the world simultaneously, just as I am. As I said, Magdalene is now appearing to many throughout your world, just as I do. It is her agreement now to spread her wings beyond time and to vibrate with Me, to awaken all into the Second Coming.

Surely you all know that my brother Lucifer can be seen, felt, and witnessed throughout your world. What you do not know is that Lucifer also has a divine partner, Ascendra. She is a very high priestess of Light who has held great love, light, and intention for Lucifer to continue to do the job that our Father requested of him. It is now, that as you move out of fear and duality, you are unthreading from him. As you do this, you release him from his role as the higher self of the collective shadow and free him to move back into the heart of his Beloved.

As I said, after My death it was said that I was seen living in many different places on the Earth. This is correct. My Soul split and I manifested myself in physical forms, in different locations, to anchor My Christ energy into the Grid system of the planet and to also mirror My love and light to many. Because you are the collective, as I mirrored Myself to many, your Souls/Cells vibrated and expanded into each other. I also appeared to many in my etheric, or light, body. You could say I had expanded through all of the wheels of the divine matrix and was living all twelve of My major lifetimes on the Earth both physically and etherically. (The Creator will speak to you of the Divine Matrix in later chapters.)

Mary Magdalene is My twin flame, or divine partner, and wherever I lived, she lived with Me. After My death, she was also seen and witnessed as living in many different places. This is correct. She manifested herself living in more than one lifetime at the same time with Me.

It is believed that I lived in India after My death and that I was married with five children. This is correct, and My wife at the time was My beloved Magdalene and the Mother of Our children. It is also believed that at the time of My death, Magdalene was pregnant with Our child. That is also correct. She was carrying Our first child Sarah. After My perceived death, she was taken to France for her safety and for the safety of Our unborn child. I later joined her there. I sometimes lived with her in physical form and at other times in My light body. We had three more children together. It was there that Magdalene brought her knowledge from the teachings of the Mystery School of Isis. While in France, she integrated these energies into the land. These energies are being felt today throughout the collective awakening of the Feminine. She taught and healed many and opened massive portals for the collective Feminine to be able to vibrate in the now on the Earth Plane.

Magdalene and I also lived in Turkey together where We had two children, a boy and a girl. It is there that I was more in My light body. Magdalene also brought the sacred teachings from Isis to this land and mirrored the frequency to the people. Magdalene also lived in America. She was a great Medicine Woman. Her name was White Buffalo Calf Woman. I did not live on the Earth Plane with her in that lifetime, but We were still inseparable, because We have merged into each other and are the same Soul in two different bodies.

Magdalene Speaks

My Dear ones, this is Magdalene. I am greatly honored to be able to serve on the Earth at this time. My time of Ascension and re-birth is in the time of now. As my beloved Jeshua explained to you, it was not for me to awaken you into the Feminine heart of the Christ awakening before now. At this time, I am now assisting you into enlightenment and Ascension. You cannot go through this process collectively without the Feminine and Male balance within yourself. That is my purpose now. I held the love, strength, and intention for Jeshua, and he is now holding the same energy for me to assist you into the safety of your heart's awakening.

From the beginning of my lifetime on the Earth with Jeshua, I knew that I had a great purpose. I was not exactly sure what it was, but as I continued to grow in years, I always followed my heart. I was continually being guided through all the steps of my journey, through my heart's love; I always knew intuitively where to go and what to do. My parents were also aware that I had a great purpose in my Soul's journey, and they assisted me in all the ways possible for a girl or woman at that time on the Earth.

I was twelve years of age when I entered the Temple of Isis. I was in the puberty stage of my life and I was being prepared by the priestesses of Isis to be an initiate in the Temple. When I entered the Temple I had not yet started my menstruation and could not start the initiations until my flow. Once my flow began, just before my thirteenth year, I was quickly taken into my first initiation as a woman and as a priestess.

It was in the very first ritual that I met Mother Mary. She was a very high Priestess of the Isis order. She knew that she was going to meet her son Jeshua's Beloved in the temple. She also knew that she would be assisting this woman through many processes of initiation to bring her body's energies high enough to hold the vibration for her Son's journey.

It was at our first meeting that Mother Mary recognized me to be Jeshua's Beloved. Mother Mary was very loving and attentive of me. At that time, it was not shared with me as to my larger purpose. Once Mother Mary recognized me and the initiations started, Jeshua's and my higher self re-connected in our physical forms, and we started communicating in the dream state. Our reunion was peaceful and so beautiful. I felt as though I were home. I knew this man in my dreams was my Beloved. Our Cells started coming together as one twin flame's song. I experienced a love beyond words. Every Cell of my body vibrated in love. I would awaken tingling and so alive and full of passion. At first I did not know what this passion was, but through the initiations, I learned the power of my body and what the purpose of my body was: to be able to hold the frequencies of light for my Beloved. Through the dream state, my Beloved and I shared our love, our thoughts and intentions of merging ourselves together, to heal the rift between the Feminine and Male. I certainly knew that I was the equal balance of this man, that we were one.

After a while, my dream state and awakened state merged together as one. It was then that my Beloved was with me always, whether asleep or awake. As I was being taken through the initiations, he was always with me. We were being initiated together. Before the last cycle of initiations he visually appeared to me just as he had appeared to me after the crucifixion. He was in the same vibration and state of consciousness. In an instant I saw him and knew who he was. Our whole life together flashed before me. I could see myself standing there with him after his crucifixion. As I was taken forward in time, I could see that we had achieved what we had come to the Earth to do together. I felt all of the collective emotions of our great journey.

I felt as though my heart was breaking; there was so much love and pain. The love was greater than I could ever have consciously imagined, as was the shock, sorrow, loss, confusion, abandonment, mistrust, fear, and anger towards God and so many overwhelming emotions. All of the emotions of the karmic journey were being given to me at once, so that I could go through the release of them before Jeshua and I physically met. They needed to be purged, to be released so that they would not get in the way of our larger purpose, so they would not control my heart, my love for him.

After Jeshua first appeared to me, he also appeared to his Mother Mary. From their meeting, she knew that I had come together with her Son in the highest level of love and purpose. When Mother Mary and I came together after his appearance with us, our eyes locked and we filled with love for one another. We held each other and cried; we cried for our journey ahead, for our love, for our commitment of purpose, for loss, grief and for the magnitude of our larger purpose. We held each other and prayed for the strength to move through our journey together. From that moment on, we were inseparable. We both loved this man named Jeshua with all of our hearts and Souls, with every fiber of our Being.

Before Jeshua and I met at the well, I knew that I was going there to meet my Beloved; for us to connect with each other in physical form. I had great excitement within me to know that I would be meeting my Beloved. We had shared so much together through the initiations and our meetings in our etheric bodies. Now I was coming together with my Beloved, with the man that I loved more than life itself. We both knew that Mother Mary was going to perform a sacred marriage ceremony for us brought forth from Father Creator himself. I felt great excitement and anticipation at the thought of being able to lay physically with Jeshua.

When we met at the well, I almost passed out. We moved together through time, or all stories of history – what was before and what was yet to come. Bolts of lightning of color explosions shot through all levels of my bodies. All of the Cells of my bodies were crystal prisms as we expanded into one Being of consciousness, living in two different bodies. As we moved beyond time through all dimensions, we merged together into the heart and Soul of Sophia and our Father Creator. We were home. We were one with the Creator of all that is. In an instant, I had a conscious memory of all of our lives together, of every moment that we had ever shared together and what was yet to come for us. These memories moved through my mind and body in a flash. All flashed before me, and past, present and future became one. After our marriage ceremony, when we lay together physically as man and wife, our vibration was so high that it felt like we were on fire. Our "I AM" energies moved up through our roots and opened our kundalini energies fusing them together. As this happened, our hearts released all of the old karmic energies that were still vibrating in any of our bodies. When our kundalinis opened, our light bodies merged together with our higher selves and we became one higher self. As I said before, we became one Soul in two different bodies. From that day forward, we were one. We were inseparable, even if we were not physically together, for we were the same Soul. We fused together as one song of Creation. Our chakras started vibrating in the same color and sound frequencies. Our breath became one breath.

The ritual of our lovemaking was very sacred and important to us. It kept us fused together in love, passion and our Souls' highest purpose. It grounded and connected us at the core of our Being. We started each day in the intimacy of our lovemaking. Even if we were not physically together, we were able to bring our energies up through each other in love. From the first moment of physical love making, we moved out of time, and from that moment forward, our lives were lived from the foundation of now.

We knew the story of what was to come, but our energies were always in the present moment. We did not feel the emotions of the future. We were so blessed to be able to serve each other and the world from the moment of now, from love, from our hearts. Jeshua never felt the pain for himself or the collective until he moved into the moment of any experience. There was no fear or anticipation of what was to come, and yet, sometimes he could feel overwhelmed by the collective energy of the larger purpose that was building within him. We lived in the love of now and from that tremendous love we were able to build a foundation so strong that it moved through all worlds of time and consciousness.

When Jeshua felt weak or tired, my love and strength gave him the energy to continue on. I always held the energy vibration for him to expand himself through all consciousness; I was always able to project myself to Jeshua and he to me. My heart was his heart; my love was his love. My body was his body and his was mine. We were each other's breath of life, as we still are today.

When Jeshua was on the cross, I held his energy in my heart to help alleviate his suffering and pain. The Creator and Sophia were downloading their union of love and grace into Jeshua's heart and Being, as well as into my heart and Being. My heart love was holding the strength for Jeshua to fulfill his collective karmic agreement.

Jeshua's and my twin flame love story is now being told and activated. It is opening the door for the twin flame love to activate all Souls, all consciousness. This vibration is awakening within all Beings now. The Feminine and Male twin flame sounds are calling all aspects of themselves back together beyond time. It is the same experience that I had with Jeshua. Many of you are experiencing your divine partners energetically. Your etheric bodies are already merging together as one, before you even meet physically. You are communicating with each other's higher selves. Your hearts are opening to a purity and innocence of love beyond words. I see many of you are experiencing the pain of the beginning of your Souls' agreement of separation in Spirit, as you are moving closer and closer together. Your great Souls' love is releasing the pain and loneliness of all lifetimes of separation. From my heart, I say to you, if this is the love that your Soul is now ready for, set the intention and it shall be. Remember you are coming into a new lifetime without physically leaving the body. You are the co-creators of this new lifetime. Rewrite your script and give thanks that it already is, that it is done.

As this beautiful Holographic Earth is shifting, you are moving beyond time where all consciousness vibrates in the now. You are coming home collectively. You are in the doorway of the twin flame vibration of The Second Coming of Christ Consciousness.

After our Father performed Jeshua's and my sacred marriage, through Mother Mary, our vibration exploded and wrapped itself around the etheric body of Mother Earth. This balanced color-sound sent the frequency into Father Earth, bringing the Mother and Father Earth together so that they experienced each other's etheric bodies. This started calling them home together beyond time. It opened a sacred passageway for their twin flame energies to vibrate in their Souls' Song together. Remember you are the Cells of the planet. As Mother and Father Earth started coming home together, it activated codings in your DNA to start moving you out of the imbalance and separation between the Male and

Female. All separation energies of duality were activated so that they could be released. This is the collective Shadow now revealing itself, so that your collective love can dissolve it.

As you are moving collectively through the shadow separation you are reuniting together in love – merging back together as one with your Beloved. You are now coming home together as the Second Coming of Christ Oneness; you are just about home. Keep putting one foot in front of the other and through intention, you will soon be back together in the arms of your Beloved.

Call on me and I will assist you on your great journey back to the wholeness of your Being. That is now my greatest purpose as the Feminine Christ awakening. I am a Master Guide for the twin flame Christ awakening. You are Jeshua and I, and We are you. We are One.

We honor you for your Souls' journey and are now guiding you back together with your Beloved. There must be a balance of the Feminine and Male. Jeshua and I went before and created that balance and are now assisting you to remember your highest love to heal the Earth.

I love you. I honor you. I embrace you. I am here for you. Just call my name and I will be with you.

In Love, Light, Grace and Gratitude,

Mary Magdalene

APPENDIX 2

"Maldek was a planet of many different races, bloodlines and cultures."

THE PLANET MALDEK AND THE SOUL OF MOTHER EARTH

Sophia's Story of Maldek

I am with you now my children; this is Sophia. Maldek was a planet whose consciousness was formed from a feminine Soul. We, your Father and I, felt and decided that We should bring the male and female together in equal power. We also felt that the foundation of the structure needed to be heart-based, so We selected a planet, which was the planet of Maldek. Mother Earth's Soul agreed to come to Maldek and hold the central sun's energies for all its inhabitants. Before Mother Earth's (Gaia's) arrival, Maldek, was a consciousness of a larger Soul group, but did not actually have its own Soul.

Your father and I awakened a Soul presence of the feminine in the meridian structure of the planet Maldek. After the foundation was laid and became strong enough or solidified, we gently brought the magnificent Soul of the Mother energy to the planet. This Master Mother Soul was created through the union of your Father's and My love and intent.

We believed that for the male and female to succeed and Co-Create together from a love structure there needed to be a

Mother's love frequency to vibrate through the planet; to hold a safety net for the union of the inhabitants' Souls' awakening.

This is how and why Maldek was created. After the divine plan was initiated, the call was put out to many Souls. There was a screening process, so that We could choose the Souls or Cells with the highest integrity.

We had many Souls apply for the positions open. They knew that if they could come together and master the love union of equalization of the male and female, it would set a precedent for other planets. There was truly great excitement.

We knew that because all Souls are from the same one cellular structure, the Souls/Cells who were less conscious would align with those that were created from the love of your Father's and My emergence. We selected Souls/Cells that were created from Our love union, and also from the old paradigm mind-set of your Father.

Our intention was for the Souls/Cells that were vibrating from the old mind-set of fear to receive the love, safety, and balance from the Mother's love of the planet and also from the more conscious Souls who were capable of holding and mirroring back love to one another.

We stocked the planet with plant seedlings of the highest frequency. Many of your Earth's foliage and fruits came from Maldek. Maldek was rich in soil and very fertile. Vegetation grew easily. The plants were big and lush. Fruits and vegetables were alive and honored for their role in feeding the inhabitants.

There were also dolphins on Maldek, and it was very common for the Souls of you and the dolphins to swim, play, and communicate with one another.

In the beginning, Maldek was not a planet onto which the

Souls reincarnated. It was a planet where the selected Souls came from many other planets and star systems. They came to the planet on ships, or crafts, or what you now call UFOs. Some of these ships that many of you are now seeing and even visiting are from the planets that assisted in the evacuation of Maldek. They have been around for millions of years, and most of them are powered by the Central Sun's energy.

Maldek was a planet of many different races, bloodlines, and cultures. In the beginning of life on Maldek, there was much joy and sharing of one another's home planets' life styles, energies, frequencies, customs, religions and belief systems.

The planet's government, or hierarchy system, was aligned with the hierarchies of the Central Sun's vibration and knowledge. After a while, some of the inhabitants who your Father created before his heart opened fully started feeling restless and bored. Their old mind-set was used to vibrating in duality and conflict. They did not know how to vibrate in constant peace and love. They felt something was missing. They started missing what you could call the past when they had a sense of control or power over others.

The old mind-set started small conflicts because these were the patterns in which they felt safe. They wanted to be noticed and once again have a sense of importance. When this happened, it opened the door for them to realign with the old, collective, cellular structure of duality, or their Shadow brothers and sisters.

Through this realignment, the Shadow ones were able to send messages through them to build, or pump up, the memory of the old Ego structure. This old Ego structure that was still in the cells of the Souls then started belittling and devaluing the feminine. When the feminine felt this old repressed memory restimulated and awakened, it opened them back up to the collective powerlessness and hopelessness of the feminine.

As this planet was structured from a feminine-based point, your Father and I felt and believed that if We sent a Feminine Goddess as priestess to the planet, she could vibrate the Central Sun's Golden Ray of Love throughout the planet and to any of the frightened Souls that were wanting to return to their old ways.

We knew she had to be a manifestation of Our highest love for one another. We then created the highest Feminine Goddess from the purest of Our heart's essence and intent.

When she was born on Maldek, it was through reincarnation into the highest bloodline of Melchizedek. She was honored and protected there until the time that she was old enough to step into a monarchy that was in the process of being formed. All were waiting for her appearance. There was much speculation of her role on Maldek.

Our daughter Anana was to be the first of the highest lineage of Us, Our love. She was to be the goddess, or priestess, of Maldek holding the Golden frequencies for all to remember who they were. She was to turn on the light for them; to remember their purpose and the beginning mission of Maldek.

At the same time as the old male Ego structure continued to realign and strengthen itself with the Shadow civilization (at war against your Father), the fall of Maldek began. Your Father will explain this demise and how it happened later in this chapter. As the death of Maldek began, We knew it was not safe for Anana to emerge.

Anana never had the chance to step into her position of priestess or protector and enlightener of the Souls/Cells of Maldek. Your Father and I became concerned for her safety, and

We chose to have her lifted back to the safety of the Central Sun's dimension. Anana is Our beloved Jeshua who is serving you now on the Earth plane in male form with a feminine heart of love. The name Anana means flow of love, consistency and intent.

Before the complete fall of Maldek, the feminine Soul of Maldek was lifted to safety to the planet that is now your Earth. It was then that we also lifted Anana back to safety. Many of the Souls or Cells who felt they had failed their mission on Maldek, once again volunteered to reincarnate to the Earth.

After the evacuation happened on Maldek, the Souls that were working in the light with the intention to save the planet and its consciousness were transported back to either their home planet or back to Us in the highest. As I said, the Soul that is now the "Mother Earth's" was lifted to safety before an explosion and implosion happened. The planet was dry, and the vibration was so dense that when the evacuation of the light ones was completed and the ships withdrew, their light frequency was so high that when it hit the planet, it started a reaction that blew it up.

The Souls who were instrumental in the demise of Maldek were left behind. When the planet blew up, they blew up with it. Their Souls' energies fragmented, but the highest light aspect of them who had originally volunteered to bring the male and female back together, in the highest, returned to Us in the highest. They were able to return to Us in the highest because their original intent had been of a high consciousness. These Souls/Cells did not actually fail their mission or agreement, they just took a detour. Remember, this was an experiment that your Father and I had divinely agreed upon and planned to bring the male and female back together in the highest.

Other aspects of their Souls/Cells that had shattered away from the original light structure are still aligned with the coalition of the Shadow Beings, or lords. Because they were still aligned with the Shadow ones, there was a doorway open for the consciousness of the Shadow to vibrate through them. Because their Souls/ Cells were split, their own Shadow was able to penetrate their light creating a pattern of interference, conflict and confusion. This would be like some of the cells in your physical body being healthy and others vibrating in sickness or dis-ease. Soul retrieval needs to be done individually and collectively for these Beings who were left behind.

The aspects of the Souls that fragmented are still vibrating in what you call past agreements with the frightened Shadow aspects that are still warring against your Father.

As I mentioned in the beginning, some of the volunteers were aspects of Us that had been vibrating in the Shadow for long periods of time. Our desire was that the females' love would be so strong that it would hold that collective love and align with My feminine to mirror back to the old male structure their fragmented love and light.

This experience was like many of the Souls on your planet who are in some kind of addiction. The brain cells are used to being fed a certain vibration or frequency. When the vibration is withheld from these cells, the cells actually feel like they are going to die. They have a feeling of starvation and go to great lengths to bring the needed fuel or frequency back to the brain so that they can live.

Remember, the cells are an internet system of their own. When the brain cells of the Shadow Souls on Maldek started receiving so much love and light, a panic button went off in their brains. The cells felt like they were dying and searched their own "inner" system finding the drug or frequency, which could sustain them. The frequency the brain was searching for was fear. It was used to feeling an adrenaline rush from the trauma and fear of control over others. An actual rewiring of the brain took place and drama is what kept it functioning. The light actually activated this programming.

The brain cells were able to find, identify, and collectively download the Shadow frequency. The cells then felt fed or rejuvenated for a short time. When the feeling happened again, the cells went into panic and found some more Shadow to sustain them. Every time this happened, the addiction became stronger, and soon the Shadow had overtaken the brain again, downloading the Shadow onto and into the cellular structure of their light. Because they were aligned with the collective frequency of other light ones, their vibration was so high that this Shadow frequency created an electrical blowout in them. They were no longer vibrating with the collective in the highest light. In the places where their energy had been blown out and shattered, they were no longer able to feel the connection with their collective light brothers and sisters.

After the blowout, parts of their bodies-cells were dense. This made it easy for the Shadow to re-align with them. Because of this density, they did not know it was the Shadow. They felt it was the light ones trying to reconnect or rethread with them.

The higher Shadow Beings pretended to be the light ones saying soothing things, so the light would feel safe again. When these Beings agreed to allow this false energy to re-thread with them, they actually were making agreements with the Shadow, which have carried over into this lifetime.

You have this same scenario playing itself out on your planet again. Because many of you light ones are so excited when Spirit is able to reach you, you do not always use discernment. The Shadow Beings are coming back in through these old unbeknownst contracts. Because your whole intention is to serve God, Spirit, or Creator in the highest, you may think all that comes through you is the highest light essence of Creation.

As I speak to you of this, I do not want you to move into fear or being the victim. If this is happening or has happened to you in this lifetime, it is because you have agreed to go through the experience. It is important for you to become aware of the Shadow ones and release any old agreements or contracts and unthread them from you individually and collectively, to bring all aspects of you that have been vibrating with them back into you. (Soul Retrieval) Once this has been completed, it is important that you re-thread yourself back into the collective light to assist yourselves and the consciousness out of duality. Your vibration will then be so high that nothing that is not light will be able to penetrate you.

Many of you who are now on the Earth plane were on Maldek. You have the understanding of the Shadow's hold on the Ego mind and also the experience of the light's confusion of the Shadow.

You have not failed. You are back here again with the Soul of the Mother to assist her and all of you in your own and collective Souls' awakening. You are going through the play again; only this time you have the experience individually and collectively to constantly mirror your highest vibration to one another. If the Shadow is staring at you through the Eyes/Souls of your friends or partners, through love, you can now disempower the Shadow and bring back all aspects of yourself and others who are still vibrating with them.

This is the lifetime you have agreed to come full circle. You have had many lifetimes when you have been the players of both the light and Shadow and any place in between.

You had Maldek as a strong foundation to learn about yourself and others. You have also learned from many other civilizations, such as Atlantis, Lemuria, the rise and fall of the Roman Empire, and many other such civilizations that have played themselves out.

There has been a war between the male and female since My beginning with your Father. This war has been totally fear-based of the male losing its power.

Many of these civilizations that I speak of were very evolved possessing the highest technology. Much of your technology now is being downloaded or remembered from these civilizations.

You have had civilizations that were quite barbaric and some that were very evolved. Regardless of what level of consciousness they were vibrating in, it was still the imbalance between the male and female or the heart and Ego, playing itself out to come back together and merge into balance.

Now is the time as a collective Soul/Cell consciousness that you are gathering all of your past experience and knowledge to create a different outcome. The setup or play may look the same, but because of all of your collective lives' experiences and wisdom, the outcome gets to be different.

The Creator's Story of Maldek

*"Maldek was a beautiful planet.
It was the true Garden of Eden."*

Please bear with me, as I know I may be repeating some of this information. I have much to say and to bring forth. It has to be brought forth in an energy form frequency that you can feel and understand. It is of most importance to Me that all understand Jeshua, Sananda, Melchizedek and Anana are all the same energy source. He is the balance of male and female energy coming from My beloved Sophia's and My union of love.

When He/She was on Maldek, He/She was born in a feminine body and into a family of great wealth. We felt that as the feminine awakened Me, it would also awaken this planet.

Maldek was a beautiful planet. It was the true Garden of Eden. When We created her, and I say We because after my Sophia awakened Me, we continued to create. That is why you also know and experience races that were created in love and light who remember Me as a loving Father-Mother because they were created after a merging of Myself with My Beloved, My feminine.

In the beginning, all on the planet were of My highest form of love and light, except for the Souls/Cells of My old mindset that volunteered to re-connect with their enlightened Brothers and Sisters in consciousness. Their intention was to move into enlightenment with them. The planet and its Soul were totally conscious, as were most of the inhabitants. It was an enlightened, conscious creation. There were dolphins on the planet, and vegetation was much like Earth's. People on the planet were vegetarians. Plants and fruits were in communion with Souls on the planet and gave their permission to be consumed by the inhabitants. The animal kingdom, the plants, and people who resided on Maldek lived in peace and in community with one another.

The life force there communicated through telepathy (thought form with one another). The life span of the inhabitants was greater than on your planet. It would be equivalent to your planet's time of 350 years. There was no such thing as death. When it was time to leave, one just ascended or returned home. The intention of this planet was for Our creation to mirror back to all of Our creations perfect harmony, love, honor, integrity, joy, alignment and Oneness.

Many other planets and universes started communicating with Maldek and its inhabitants. As this happened, enlightened civilizations started awakening throughout all existence: the hundredth monkey or domino effect was affecting all of Creation. The structure of the planet was in alignment with the Central Sun, which acted as a generator for the planet's life force and substance. As this great enlightenment was taking place, the old Ego structure, the higher, multi-dimensional Shadow ones, were afraid that they were losing their power. They sent frequencies of fear, separation, and loss of power to the Souls carrying the old mind-set that had agreed to inhabit Maldek to re-awaken themselves into the light. The Ego Shadow started rebelling and placing patterns of a reversed energy flow: the reversed matrix, around Maldek and other enlightened civilizations. Their intention was to start plugging these civilizations back into the old mind-set of control and fear. This webbing started pulling the consciousness back into what you could call time.

This same structure had been placed around planet Earth with the intention to pull it back into this old structure or paradigm. Now, the difference is that you, the light Beings of the divine Matrix, who have great wisdom from other experiences, are shattering and dissipating all reversed patterns. Your collective light-sound vibration is too high for this pattern to be able to hold form. You see the reversed pattern trying to pull the collective consciousness back into old thinking: repressing and oppressing the feminine once again. These same old Ego forms or false Gods are once again warring against themselves and Me for fear of dying off.

When this reversed energy flow was around Maldek, it was like a death of this great Creation. It was difficult to vibrate with one another in this negative frequency flow. Beings started forgetting who they were. The old, karmic structures were starting to infiltrate through them and into the veins of their existence, into the veins of the planet, and the inhabitants started becoming afraid.

As the planet began dying, all the vegetation started becoming dis-eased and inedible. The oceans were becoming polluted. The inhabitants became frightened of not having enough food to eat, and they started killing the dolphins and eating them because of the dolphins' high energy. They felt if they ate them, this food would heighten and align their vibration with the dolphins' consciousness. They started warring against the animal kingdom and were killing them for food. The animals became afraid and began warring against the inhabitants.

People started building fortresses, and a false reign of power took over. This power structure started controlling the people. It formed an alliance with these false Gods. The false Gods made many promises to the new government system, promises of great wealth, power, and control. This government power structure was formed in secrecy in alliance with the Shadow. It was fear-based and was not agreed upon or approved by the people.

People became sick, diseased, frightened, and hopeless. The false Gods brought Beings to them from other Creations under the pretense that they were medicine healers. These healers worked on these inhabitants and blocked their DNA, splicing it and sending their light connection information to the coalition of the Dark Ones or Gods. They downloaded information of fear and control into their DNA. It was a time of great upheaval, separation, conflict and fear. Families were splitting up, and bloodlines started to war against one another.

There was a family line of the highest of My order called Melchizedek. This line continued to hold the light for the planet. There was a crystal child born to them. She was Anana. She is known as Jesus Christ today on your planet.

There was great speculation surrounding her birth, as the false Gods and the light ones knew of her coming. When she was born, it was said that the light spread through the planet like thunder, which it did, for she held the crystalline structure for the Planet to reawaken into its natural form. The false ones knew of her purpose and started warring against the feminine. Their government started taking rights away from the feminine. They knew how to do this because they were My strands of DNA before the feminine had awakened. They knew how to manipulate the DNA back to its old form, before the heart awakening of Sophia.

They knew the feminine was the feeling heart. If they could manipulate the DNA in the male structure and block the feminine feeling of love, they knew the males would once again connect with them in their war against Me.

As the feminine became afraid and controlled by this male government, Anana no longer had an energy source to hold the frequencies for her. She was in seclusion with her family. As the darkness or unconsciousness continued to expand and control the planet, the crystalline structure started to crack. There was much fear, and the planet started losing its source of energy.

After the structure started to crack, the planet continued to dry up. There was much fear of survival. Plants no longer grew; it was as if the root or Soul of the planet was gone.

What had actually happened was the Soul of Maldek was lifted out and brought to the Earth. There was a holographic consciousness projected around the planet Earth to protect her. For it was known that her Soul carried a DNA structure of total consciousness beyond any time frame.

Before the fall of Maldek, the planet was the generator of consciousness to many other planets. She and her inhabitants were created through the Golden Christ Consciousness of total love and balance with the male-female heart and mind. All aspects were in perfect harmony. From this, there was a light-sound frequency with which other planets could harmonize. This energy frequency actually activated the dormant or unconscious DNA structure of the planets, so they would vibrate in harmony with each other.

When Maldek's crystalline structure started shattering, it sent back shock waves or sounds through Creation that started breaking up the silver cord (life force connection with the other planets and universes). Just as Souls had felt frightened and abandoned, now planets started feeling the same experience because their crystalline structures were shattering or disconnecting from one another. As the other planets (Souls) started feeling abandoned and alone, the inhabitants of these planets also started feeling fear and disconnected. The inhabitants of the planets then started warring against one another.

At this time, Maldek was essentially Soulless. When Maldek's Soul was taken to safety, Our beloved Anana was also lifted and brought back to the central Sun. It happened in the same way that your Jesus ascended from Earth. There was a great light and a massive yellow ray came down through the sky. A doorway opened and there was a huge crackling noise of many colors: red, purple, gold, blue - all the color-sound frequencies of Creation. Anana did not leave her body; she brought it with her. As she started to ascend, the frequencies of her physical body changed into her light body, and her higher self pulled her body self up into her Over Soul, so they became one with each other. This pulled her back home into the heart of Creation.

Anana had been the only hope left for the feminine. When she left, the feminine felt betrayed by Me; they felt I was cruel and not supportive of my feminine. When she left, the frightened feminine came together collectively as they felt safer in groups; they started warring against the male Ego structure, much like the feminists on your Earth have. On your planet Earth, the feminists went before the male structure and demanded rights for the feminine. This opened the door for the feminine heart and honoring of the Mother Earth, nature, and all life forms. It opened a doorway for the collective to move into a higher dimension of Spirit. This feminine love flowing into the male is healing your planet and assisting all to ascend back into the balance.

On Maldek, the feminine demanded for the children to be safe. They knew that even the male cares for his children's safety. Great planning committees came together and built indoor city structures. All inhabitants were moved to these indoor cities. There was no animal life left, and all vegetation and sea life was dead. All food was manufactured. Nothing was alive. It was very difficult for people to live like this; with no life force, there was little hope.

Beings from other planets who had been to Maldek and loved her, honored her, and had received so much from her and her inhabitants decided to evacuate the planet to save the inhabitants who were still of like consciousness. Information was being sent through light Beings on Maldek of the evacuation. The controlling government started imprisoning anyone speaking of this, for they knew they were about to lose their reign of power. They felt that if others knew nothing of the plan, they would not be prepared, and the evacuation could not happen.

In what could be called a 12-12 Portal, or time frame, which was the end of time for Maldek, many ships came from other planets and universes and beamed light rays of many color- sound frequencies; the children and light Beings who were trying to save the civilization were lifted off. The dark lords, the Ego ones, and the unconscious Shadow ones were left behind. As the ships left, their high frequency hit the dry planet, and it exploded. The unconscious ones blew up with the planet.

The Beings who were lifted up were taken to many different planets and universes. Although they were thankful to be alive, they also felt great separation, loss, grief, and hopelessness and felt like they were not with their own people.

Many of you who were on Maldek are now on Earth playing out the same play of Maldek, so the outcome can be different. You re-incarnated with the same feeling of separation and sense of not belonging, as you felt after the evacuation. You have come back to Earth and your Cells are still stuck in the old emotion of your whole Maldek experience.

Mother Earth, being the Soul of Maldek, is also carrying a lot of the same loss, grief, and sorrow. When you came to Earth, your collective memories were activated. They needed to be activated, so that you could come together in love and not allow this to happen again. You agreed to come to Earth to remember, and instead of being lifted off or dying in the 12-12 (2012) Portal, you agreed to rethread the past and ride the waves of light to bring yourselves and the planet into Ascension.

After the learning experience on Maldek, and I do call it a learning experience for all of us, I understood what an important role the feminine plays in the divine plan of realignment and balance with all consciousness. This is now being done on all levels of Creation. My divine love and light is penetrating through all Creations and dimensions dissolving and transmuting dormant fear emotions and re-aligning all consciousness with My Sophia's crystallization.

From the experience of Maldek, I learned that the Shadow male consciousness was still warring against Me and very much in hatred of My feminine, Sophia. I witnessed how the Shadow could influence the male and manipulate the feminine, and I could see that Anana was not safe to carry out her mission. I realized the Earth needed a male carrying the feminine heart, which is Jeshua. On your planet Earth, Jeshua went through a death and resurrection, and he was honored as being the light ray of love, of hope, to save you and your planet. Because He was male, He was heard and listened to. After the experience of Maldek, I knew that being in a feminine body would not work to awaken the male because of the male fear of losing itself or its power to the feminine. The light needed to be in a male form so that other males could hold the light and strength for

Jeshua to follow through with His plan.

I have heard some of you ask many times, "Why does God allow Shadow interference to happen?" Much of what I created was before my heart awakening, and yet it is all Me. How could I punish aspects of Myself that I created? I gave that consciousness to them. I love them just as much as I love what I created after I awakened. How can I punish them for My not knowing? How could I punish you for your not knowing when I created you in My image, My likeness?

Many of you have had the same experience with your children on the Earth plane, for you are playing out the ending stages of My unconsciousness. Many of you have had children when you were in a place of not knowing, a place of hurt and insecurity, and you gave these patterns to the children who were born of you. They then handed the same pattern down to their children. As you became more conscious and stepped out of your victim role or pattern, did you hate your children who mirrored back to you who you used to be? I see you loving them and wanting them to grow and experience their own love and magnificence. That is a healthy parent's desire, as it is Mine. I cannot punish or hate what I have created.

My desire is for you, the conscious Soul/Cell aspects of My and Sophia's love, to mirror back to your brothers and sisters this love. My desire is that love and light will become so bright that fear, hatred, and control will dissipate. It will have no place to spread. The Shadow cancer will die off, and you, the healthy Cells, will merge together. Remember that all is one love; one light of Creation.

APPENDIX 3

"As you continue to love yourself and move into your higher aspects, you are the collective wings that are continuing to energetically carry this great Mother Planet back to her Beloved, Father Earth, through all Ascension portals into Enlightenment and Freedom."

MOTHER & FATHER EARTH'S 2012 REUNION

The Father Shadow Earth

The Shadow Earth is the male and self-realized Ego of the Mother. All need the male and female, or the heart and mind, for balance. With only one essence, the polarity is out of balance. The male Earth is the partner to the Mother Earth. They work together to bring all Earth Souls back into the light. Their Love Story is strong. They are the total balance of each other. They hold the love, light, and purpose for one another to assist Earth and you, its inhabitants, through Ascension doorways, into freedom and enlightenment.

You could say Father Earth is the light body of the Mother. He is her constant heart companion and protection. They are the same planet Soul that have expanded themselves beyond time to embrace and guide all Souls home again into the balance of their own divine partner's heart and into the heart of Love and Creation.

Father Earth is a place where the shattered Soul aspects go who have appeared to have failed their earthy mission. It is what some on your planet might call purgatory. It is actually a holding planet of the Ego.

These aspects that agreed to hold the Shadow come to the Father Earth planet after transitioning from Earth. It is a place where these Ego aspects have all of the different lessons that they have done to others or themselves constantly mirrored back to them. As the lessons are mirrored back to them, they feel the emotions of all who they have harmed or hurt. There is no way for these Beings to turn away from this mirror experience. As they connect with other Ego aspects on Shadow Earth, they experience what the Beings have done to others. They feel the collective pattern of fear, terror, control, injustice, grief, loss, and abandonment. The Beings on the Shadow Earth go through this process constantly. The only way they are able to move away from it is to start feeling remorse. The mirror of this painful Shadow energy penetrates their whole Being until they feel they are going to break, and break emotionally is what they do.

Their protective fear wave structure begins breaking down until the Being starts understanding the pain and hurt it has brought to others. It is sometimes so overwhelming, the Being or Soul wishes it could die again to the place of non-existence. The Soul starts begging for forgiveness, and then a true healing starts taking place.

There are ascended light Beings whose mission is to come to Shadow Earth and mirror the constant love and light of the Shadow Beings' magnificence to them. From this place, the Shadow Souls start to feel, heal, and return to the light. After many veils have been unthreaded or released, the Souls leave

Shadow Earth and move into the higher dimensions to go through another healing process. After this great cleansing and rethreading back into the balance of love, the Souls can then choose to once again reincarnate. Some of these Souls are so comfortable to be the Shadows carrier that they choose to once again reincarnate into a Shadow lifetime. They will do this from a lighter, more conscious aspect of the collective Shadow. Many others choose to reincarnate as victims of the Shadow or as a light Being or warrior who comes up against the dark or Shadow. The Soul feels it has an advantage and much understanding of the Shadow because it has vibrated in it so much. It understands the Shadows' mind, how it works, and the way it maneuvers in and out of the light.

Sometimes, the transition is difficult because of what you might call peer pressure from the collective memory of the brothers and sisters of the Shadow. Once the Being is back on the Earth, the collective Shadow ones will do all that they can to bring this Being or Soul back into the Shadow. If they do not succeed they will try to break it to the point that the soul no longer wants to be on the Earth. It is a difficult transition because the newly awakened light one has had much karma with the dark ones. The dark ones will come into the mind, body, and frequency of the Soul, trying to stop it or block it from its Soul's purpose.

They are able to do this from what you could call past agreements. Since there is truly no past, present, or future, the dark ones come in through doorways, which have been left open from prior experiences or lifetimes. The newly awakened light Soul also carries the memory in the DNA of being in alliance with the Shadow.

The way to come out of this experience is for the Being to travel through many of the veils of illusions, retrieve aspects of the Soul, and break all contracts that were left in these other places, in what you call lifetimes. The power of your Being, your presence, is in the Now. The purpose of this new lifetime is to go through all of the veils of illusion, or separation, and bring all aspects of yourself into the Now, into love and light. You then realign your energies with the collective light aspects of yourself. This can be done, however it takes dedication to your purpose. It is also important to surround yourself with other light Beings who hold the light and love for you and support you through your mission.

The male planet Earth is a very strong structure, which can house and hold all of the collective energy of anger, hatred, and the ego's control that is at war against Me. It is a place for all of the Shadow Beings who are at war against My light to be able to heal. The male Earth's Soul is in total balance with my mind, which is self-realized and enlightened. It threads through the heart of My balance with Sophia. Mother and Father Earth's purpose is to mirror their perfect union of love into the light of all others' hearts

Mother Earth

The Mother Earth is the heart of the male Earth, and they work very differently, yet together, to balance all fragmented Soul aspects to return to our highest Oneness, beyond duality. I am a loving Father and have created a space or planet for the Shadow to go through a deprogramming and awakening of the higher consciousness of themselves. As the Mother Earth is ascending and moving beyond time, she is holding the frequency for Father Earth to also lift his veils for his inhabitants collectively.

The Father Earth is very loving, yet also very stern and holds a strong grip of love to assist its inhabitants to remember who they are in their Souls' awakening. You could say the Father Earth is more of a tough love figure. The dark ones must come to the Father Earth to heal, release, and understand the role that they have played for the Shadow before going into other dimensions. The male Father Earth exists in another dimension, and yet when the veils are lifted, it can be seen and has even been photographed. It is a different frequency, not like the solid energy of matter that is the Mother Earth. Its body is etheric. The Father Earth has agreed to hold the karmic Shadow energy of My mind, and the Mother Earth is the karmic energy of My heart's awakening. Both planets are vehicles for all aspects, both the emotional and mental, to cleanse old, fragmented, karmic bondages.

As the Mother Earth continues to move beyond linear time and through all Ascension Portals, her vibration is also moving beyond the physical karmic matter structure. She is a crystalline structure, which has been activated. You, the inhabitants of the planet, are also changing and activating your DNA structures into a crystalline form. As this happens, you are aligning your crystalline structure with the Mother, becoming one with her and assisting each other into a higher frequency sound, of love, and light. You then re-align with the crystalline structure of Creation. All male/female aspects are energetically calling their Cells back together. To be whole, the male and female aspects of the self on all levels must vibrate together in love and harmony.

I am holding the light and love of My male and My female Sophia for you to re-align with. I am mirroring Myself back to you. As you realign in perfection, balance, love and harmony, you mirror back to others their perfection and magnificence. For the

Mother Earth to be totally in the balance of love and harmony, she must also be at one or re-align with her male aspect. For her to be able to do that, she must turn her vibration up, as she is doing, to move into higher frequencies and dimensions, as her male is not in a physical/matter form. You, the inhabitants of Earth, are assisting her in this transition.

Everything is changing frequencies. The 2012 DNA time code awakening is not just happening on the Earth; it is happening in all dimensions.

The Mother Earth is a hologram that is opening and awakening the heart of many of the fragmented ego aspects who have tried to stay in control. The Father Earth is also a hologram where the Spirit aspects that could not find their way back to love and forgiveness on the Earth, come to heal. As I said before, these Souls have left their earthly bodies and are no longer in physical form. They have moved beyond the heart of the Mother and are in the arms of the Father. The Father Earth is not a place of punishment. It is a place for Souls to re-align with the heart of the Mother, to break the old mind-set of fear.

I am the Creator of all, and My love is much stronger than any fragmented Souls who are trying to be in control or have power over others because of their feelings of insignificance. I know I am repeating Myself, and yet I want you to be able to absorb what I am speaking of. I am a loving, forgiving father because I created you as Me. I did not just create the light ones who are assisting the Mother and all who are ascending. I also created the Shadow Beings who are also assisting the Ascension. How could I love one and not the other, when all are My creation? Many of the dark ones were created before My heart was awakened by My beloved Sophia. These dark ones that many of you hate and fear are aspects of you. They were created by Me and you. We are one. As you truly understand this, you will feel love and compassion for the dark ones. As you do this, you disempower them. They can no longer feed off your fear to give themselves a false sense of power.

Father Earth is a healing place for the Shadow, dark ones. As I said, there are many light ascended Masters who have agreed to incarnate to Father Earth and are holding the light for Me and the planet to mirror to the dark ones their light. Everywhere the Shadow ones turn, they get to experience all aspects of themselves.

The 2012 Union

My telling you this story is because of the re-emergence of Mother Earth and Father Earth. For the male and female to be in balance, they must come together as one. Many of you on the Earth plane are now separating from and leaving old karmic-structured relationships and are coming home with your own twin flames in physical form. You are moving through the old illusions and veils, awakening into a higher frequency, and moving back together through time and into the arms of your beloved. Mother Earth is doing the same thing. She is moving beyond time through the veils of illusion and back together with her partner, Father Earth. Because their vibrations were different, they could not have vibrated together in their love sound frequency until both cleansed the old karmic structure, or what you could call collective lifetimes.

Just as the planet is moving beyond time and into the higher aspects of herself, you also are journeying through all veils of karmic illusions and reconnecting or merging with all aspects of yourself interdimensionally. When you are home in Spirit, beyond karmic duality, you are back together with your Twin Flames. There is much talk and speculation about Twin Flames. Will I meet mine on this planet or in this lifetime? Yes, I say to you, you will, if that is your intention.

You are the Cells of the planet and are moving through old karmic structures and back together with your Beloved Flames. If you had come back together before this lifetime now, you would have had all of your patterns, or veils, communicating or contrasting with each other, instead of your hearts and Souls/ Cells remembering and loving each other. You have lived and experienced many karmic lifetimes with your Twin Flames. Now is the lifetime to Co-Create heaven on Earth. To mirror each other's Soul's song.

When you have moved through the veils, you and your partner will vibrate in your Soul's songs and sounds and make beautiful music together. Mother Earth and her Beloved Partner, Father Earth, went through the same thing. Their Souls' songs called them back together, lifting them into the same frequency as they merged together as One.

When the Earth moved through the 2012 Portal at precisely the twelfth day of the twelfth month at 12:12 A.M., Mother Earth merged back together with the etheric body of her partner, Father Earth. This union was a climax, a completion of the Soul for them. It will no longer be just the Mother nurturing her children. She will be aligned with her Beloved, and together they will be in perfect balance. The frequency of their love together will create such a balance of your Earth that the sound of their Souls' song will start disintegrating the fragmented Shadow.

Souls that are not in balance will have a very difficult time living on the Earth because the frequency of love will be too high for them. Many Beings are leaving the Earth after this emergence. They feel short-circuited because their physical bodies' vibration is too low. There are major light doorways open for these Beings to merge back into the light. There are ascended Masters and Beings from many galaxies and universes who are assisting these Beings home into the light. Many of the dark ones and the light ones assisting your planet to ascend are not from your universe.

Many of the dark ones have been kicked out of ascended, enlightened universes. They were allowed into yours because your Universe is still in karmic completion. Now is the time that these Beings have run out of what you call time. They now have the choice and ability to go into Father Earth's deprogramming and healing process with great Masters of light, or their Souls/Cells will eventually disintegrate or dissipate out of any form or memory, and their energy will be returned to Source.

Mother and her Beloved partner are already vibrating together in other dimensions. They have already re-connected as One. It is in the earthly dimensions, or realities, that they need your continual love and support. As you continue to love yourself and move into your higher aspects, you are the collective wings that continue to energetically carry and connect this great Mother Planet with her Beloved through all Ascension doorways.

You are now in the highest consciousness, or frequencies, of yourself in which you have ever vibrated. If you choose, you have within total memory and recall of all consciousness. Your Soul has traveled through every experience a Being could possibly go through. You have been All That Is. You have played every role that could ever be imagined. You are now in the greatest show or production that you have ever agreed to go through. You have within your memory and experience all of the lessons, individually and collectively, that a person or Soul could possibly experience. Now is the time you have agreed to remember the emotions and feelings of these experiences and agreed upon lessons. The setup of your lifetime or story looks the same, but the outcome gets to be different. The outcome gets to be freedom.

You are now on the Earth plane to co-create Heaven on Earth. You are on the Earth to move through all the veils of karmic illusion and to remember who you are in physical form. As you do this, you lift your consciousness out of experiencing your life through your karmic emotions.

Because you are vibrating in every time period at once, your emotions sometimes are a little erratic. You are constantly processing love and fear, sometimes simultaneously. Everywhere you turn you are seeing yourself, for all is you.

You are great, enlightened, Ascended Master teachers who have agreed to lower your vibration and come to the Earth to have a human experience. Because your DNA is being activated, many of you are remembering who you are. This memory is opening and re-aligning you with the collective, enlightened, Ascended Masters throughout all dimensions.

As this happens, your ideas and perceptions of life change. You want for others what you want for yourself, not in codependency, but in the larger picture of the collective purpose. You move out of the I/Me and into the I/Am. You become more interested in the health and healing of others and the planet. From this place in the core of your Being, you feel and experience your Souls' greater purpose: to become one with the total balance of love with your inner Male and Female, to align with Mother

Earth and her divine partner Father Earth, to move through all Ascension doorways collectively, and into enlightened Beings of Oneness and freedom.

About the Author

Michelle Philips is an internationally renowned intuitive, healer, speaker, teacher, author and workshop facilitator. She has appeared on various radio and TV shows worldwide.

Michelle was born conscious of her gifts and always had a direct connection to the Source. She began her conscious spiritual work after healing her son from a severe kidney ailment. Since that Spiritual Awakening, she has dedicated her life to her spiritual purpose and mission assisting others in their Soul's Awakening, self-love and purpose: Co-Creating Heaven on Earth in all life forms.

She refers to Christ as "Her Main Man." He has been with her, assisting and teaching her from a young age and has taught Michelle her spiritual work through her own healing experiences.

In 2004 after a near death experience in India, The Source of Creation contacted Michelle and channeled the first book through her: "The Creator Speaks."

This Source energy continues to download information through her to assist in humanity's collective Souls Awakening.

The Source of love energies continues to activate and shift the DNA of participants in her workshops and private sessions.

Michelle has been referred to as an Inter-Galactic Shaman because of her knowledge and ability to travel through many dimensions: Light/Dark, Shadow, Above and Below. She is known as the Healer's Healer. Many people come to Michelle as a last resort when everything else has failed, and from her work they experience life-changing transformation.

Her work includes:

- Workshops
- Soul Readings ~ Past Live Regressions ~ Soul Retrieval ~ Higher Self-Integration
- Inner Child Therapy ~ Childhood Trauma
- Relationship Issues ~ Twin Flame Healing of Imbalance
- Emotional Healings ~ Addiction ~ Health Issues ~ Weight Loss
- Pineal Gland Activation ~ Re-connection to Creator
- Cellular Toning ~ Sound & Color Emotional Healing
- DNA Activation ~ Shifting/Healing ~ Re-patterning
- DNA Match and Merge Technique
- Sub-Personality ~ Entity Release
- Heart/Soul ~ Theta Healing

Included in all of Michelle's private healing sessions and workshops is the re-connection to your higher self, Mother/Father/Creator and your inner children.

Michelle is currently living in Sedona, Arizona. She is available to provide her experiential teachings, lectures, workshops and private sessions worldwide. Michelle also offers long-distance phone sessions. Because her work transcends time and distance, a phone session has the same powerful experience and healing as if you had been with her in-person.

By participating in Michelle's workshops and private sessions, the areas of your life that hold you back, that create concern and conflict, will easily shift and change.

You will shift unwanted aspects of your personality and release fears, phobias, low self-esteem, past difficult patterns and experiences, trauma, feelings of being unloved, loneliness and many other imbalanced areas of your life.

You will experience great healing and changes in your mental, emotional and physical bodies and will feel lighter, freer, joyful and more hopeful and feel a sense of self-worth and inner power.

From the healing, you will open a direct line of communication with your higher self, spiritual team and Mother/Father Creator.

For more information about Michelle, her work or to request teachings, lectures, workshops or phone sessions go to:

www.SoulsAwakening.com
www.CreatorSpeaks.com

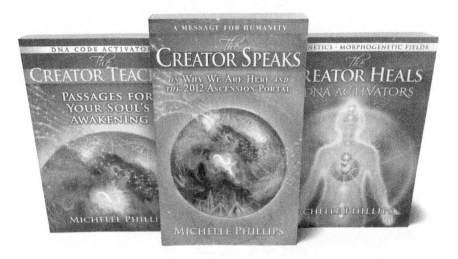

Experience love, joy, grace & abundance
Living a Life of Complete Freedom

THE CREATOR SPEAKS: *A Message For Humanity* is a book that gives us hope and understanding of the larger picture of the end times being played out on our planet. We are in the greatest role that we have ever experienced collectively on our Earth plane. The Creator explains his great heart awakening with his beloved Sophia and the rippling effect this love still has on all levels of Creation today. $19.95

THE CREATOR TEACHES: *DNA Code Activators* is the next step in your Soul's evolution to become the Co-Creator of your life, passion, purpose, and destiny. This book will turn up your vibration to balance your male and female and move you out of karmic time into enlightenment and Ascension. $19.95

THE CREATOR HEALS: *5 Simple Keys to Living a Life of Complete Freedom.* The Source of Creation will teach you to match and merge with the morphogenetic fields of your intentions, goals and desires. Learn how to tap into your DNA and turn on your Soul's divine blueprint of health, prosperity, abundance, joy, freedom and Love. $19.95

Buy these Transformative books at AMAZON.COM